CW00687098

100 WALKS IN STAFFORDSHIRE

THE CROWOOD PRESS

First published in 2017 by
The Crowood Press Ltd
Ramsbury, Marlborough
Wiltshire SN8 2HR

www.crowood.com

© The Crowood Press 2017

All rights reserved. No part of this publication may be reproduced or transmitted in any form
or by any means, electronic or mechanical, including photocopy, recording, or any information
storage and retrieval system, without permission in writing from the publishers.

British Library Cataloguing-in-Publication Data
A catalogue record for this book is available from the British Library.

ISBN 978 1 78500 347 9

Front cover: Shutterstock

Mapping in this book is sourced from the following products: OS Explorer OL24, 259;
OS Landranger 110, 118, 119, 123, 127, 128, 138, 139

© Crown copyright 2016 Ordnance Survey. Licence number 100038003

Every effort has been made to ensure the accuracy of this book. However, changes can occur
during the lifetime of an edition. The Publishers cannot be held responsible for any errors or
omissions or for the consequences of any reliance on the information given in this book, but
should be very grateful if walkers could let us know of any inaccuracies by writing to us at
the address above or via the website.

As with any outdoor activity, accidents and injury can occur. We strongly advise readers to
check the local weather forecast before setting out and to take an OS map. The Publishers
accept no responsibility for any injuries which may occur in relation to following the walk
descriptions contained within this book.

Typeset by Jean Cussons Typesetting, Diss, Norfolk
Printed and bound in India by Replika Press Pvt Ltd

Contents

How to Use this Book

Each walk in this book begins with an information panel that shows the distance, start point, a summary of route terrain and level of difficulty (Easy/ Moderate/Difficult), OS map(s) required, and suggested pubs/cafés at the start/end of walk or *en route*.

MAPS
There are 97 maps covering the 100 walks. Some of the walks are extensions of existing routes and the information panel for these walks will tell you the distance of the short and long versions of the walk. For those not wishing to undertake the longer versions of these walks, the 'short-cuts' are shown on the map in red.

The routes marked on the maps are punctuated by a series of numbered waypoints. These relate to the same numbers shown in the walk description.

Start Points
The start of each walk is given as a postcode and also a six-figure grid reference number prefixed by two letters (which indicates the relevant square on the National Grid). More information on grid references is found on Ordnance Survey maps.

Parking
Many of the car parks suggested are public, but for some walks you will have to park on the roadside or in a lay-by. Please be considerate when leaving your car and do not block access roads or gates. Also, if parking in a pub car park for the duration of the walk, please try to avoid busy times.

COUNTRYSIDE CODE
- Consider the local community and other people enjoying the outdoors
- Leave gates and property as you find them and follow paths
- Leave no trace of your visit and take litter home
- Keep dogs under effective control
- Plan ahead and be prepared
- Follow advice and local signs

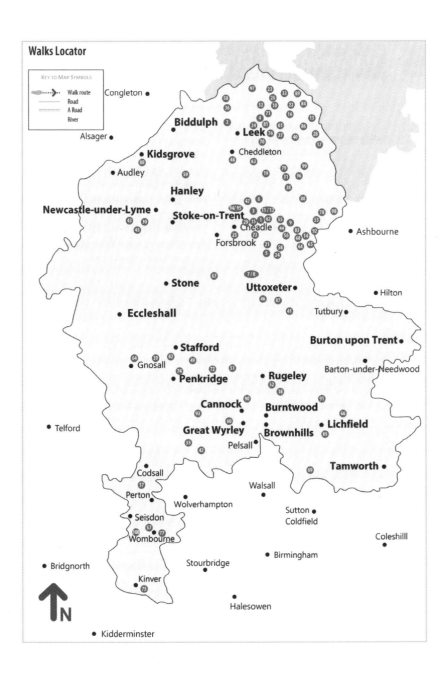

Walks Locator

KEY TO MAP SYMBOLS

- Walk route
- Road
- A Road
- River

N

Oakamoor and Dimmingsdale

START The car park near the Admiral Jervis Inn, ST10 3AG, GR 053447

DISTANCE 3 miles (5km)

SUMMARY Easy

MAPS OS Landranger 123

WHERE TO EAT AND DRINK The Ramblers Retreat, T 01538 702730, www.ramblersretreat.co.uk: open Mar–Oct Mon–Fri 10am–5pm, weekends 10am–6pm; Nov–Feb Mon–Fri 10.30am–3pm, weekends 10am–5pm
The Admiral Jervis Inn, Oakamoor, T 01538 702187, www.the-admiral-jervis-inn.com: open 1200–2300 daily

A flat path through banks of trees by the River Churnet makes this a good family walk.

[1] From the car park, go across the grassed picnic area to a footbridge over the river. Canoeists can often be seen here. This area is a credit to Staffordshire Moorlands Council, who created the picnic area from what was Bolton's Copper Works in 1962. Stone gate pillars from the railway sidings on the stone bases for heavy machinery can still be seen on the other side of the river.

[2] Cross the bridge and turn right on a wide path to a second car park. This was the site of Oakamoor Railway Station, and one of the old platforms can still be seen over on the left. Go to the end of this platform and follow a wide path marked by Staffordshire County Council as the Old Churnet Railway, which, as the name suggests, was once the railway line. Keep on this path for about 1½ miles in the Churnet Valley, passing first a local cricket field, then a football field, and finally a small lake where fishermen congregate. At the right time of year this walk offers a number of sporting scenes! Watch out for a stone bridge (Lord's Bridge) crossing above the path, and immediately in front of it look out for a plank bridge over the ditch to the left. Cross this to a narrow path leading up to the bridge.

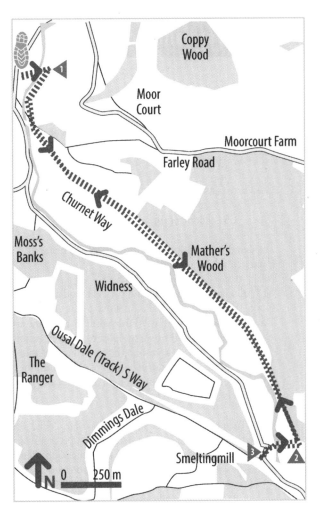

③ Turn right to cross the bridge and follow the path through to a minor road.

④ The Ramblers Retreat – which has been converted from a hunting lodge – is opposite, where refreshments may be taken either inside or out in the garden. The return is back the way you came – across the bridge and back along the Churnet Valley to Oakamoor.

Rudyard and Horton

START The Rudyard car park situated on the old railway embankment, ST13 8XB, GR 955579

DISTANCE 3 miles (5km)

SUMMARY Easy

MAPS OS Landranger 119

WHERE TO EAT AND DRINK The Rudyard Lake visitor centre café; open summer 10am–5pm Mon–Fri, weekends until 6pm; Oct–Mar weekends only 10am–5pm, but check their website www.rudyardlake.com

A delightful and scenic short walk for all the family. Horton is particularly charming.

1 Go down to the road and turn left, and at the mini roundabout take the left fork and walk for 300yd to the end of the built-up area and the speed-limit sign. At this point go up a lane and footpath, right, and cross a stile by a signpost to Horton. Follow the obvious footpath over stiles, and soon the church comes into view situated on the hill in the delightful hamlet of Horton. In the last field keep the hedgerow on your left, head up the bank and go through a gate on to a lane-cum-parking area.

2 Turn right alongside the churchyard to a road junction. Go straight across and diagonally right up a small lane past a magnificent old vicarage. Go straight ahead on a lane/footpath, and after 150yd turn right over a stile and into a field. Cross this to a squeezer and footbridge, beyond which head up another field alongside the road, following a hedgerow, until it is possible to leave by a stile on to the road. Turn left for 250yd, and at a footpath sign go right along a farm lane to Stone House. Continue in a similar direction for 300yd, past quarries in a wood, to reach a road.

3 Turn right here to go through Rudyard and back to the car park.

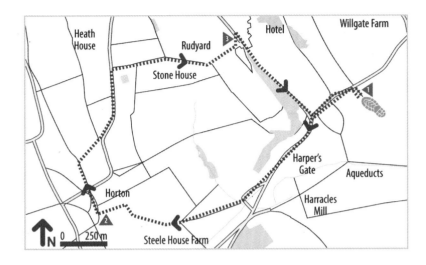

Points of interest

 Rudyard is a Victorian inland resort that is enjoying a new lease of life. Kipling's parents reputedly named him after happy memories of this place.

Dimmingsdale and Ousal Dale

START The public car park adjacent to The Ramblers Retreat café, ST10 4BU, GR 062432

DISTANCE 3¾ miles (6km)

SUMMARY Moderate

MAPS OS Landranger 119

WHERE TO EAT AND DRINK The Ramblers Retreat, T 01538 702730, www.ramblersretreat.co.uk: open Mar–Oct Mon–Fri 10am–5pm, weekends 10am–6pm; Nov–Feb Mon–Fri 10.30am–3pm, weekends 10am–5pm; prices are moderate

A fine, rugged stroll, up and round the sandstone and Bunter pebble beds of the deeply incised Churnet Valley.

1 Facing the front of the café, take the path signposted Woodland Walk veering off to the right, to reach a gradually ascending sandstone track with woods on its right. Pass an old smelting mill, a fishpond and a small lake, all on the left. Keep to the right of Earls Rock, and continue following the track upwards until eventually you come to a track.

2 Turn right over a cattlegrid. Proceed along this lane past a pond, and follow it across several fields to meet a minor road. Turn left on the road for ¼ mile down to Oldfurnace, where a track comes from the left and a lane leads off right.

3 Go on for about 50yd, and cross over the style next to a farm gate on the left. Go diagonally right uphill, keeping to the left of a gully to reach a fence. Follow the fence along to the left, to a stile. Cross over the stile on to Carriage Drive, a wide track, and go left along it for a few hundred yards until it curves left.

4 Here take the path on the right, which runs upwards. Follow this path to a stile at the top, and cross it into a field; go straight over to the corner of a coppice to join a farm track.

5 Turn right along this track; there are fine views over the Staffordshire Dales.

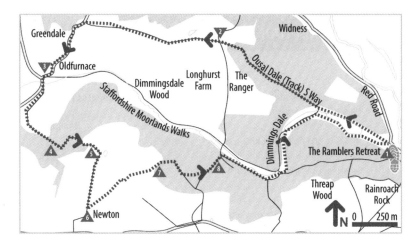

[6] Just before you reach a cottage situated on the right, go over a stile on the left next to the corner of a stone wall and into a field; take a path which almost comes back on yourself to cross the field diagonally to another stile. Cross the stile into a second field and cross to another, visible stile. In the third field turn right along the wall to a stile in a corner. Cross into a fourth, large field and go diagonally across it, passing to the right of a large oak tree. Go down to a stile in the right corner, by woods. Cross into a fifth field, keeping to the right edge to reach a stile.

[7] Cross into woods, and in a few yards keep to the right and follow a gradually descending path. At a fork bear left, going more steeply down to reach Carriage Drive again.

[8] Turn right to follow this wide track back to the Ramblers Retreat where the walk started.

Points of interest

An eighteenth-century lead smelting mill for the ores from Ecton.

Hawksmoor Nature Reserve

START The layby at High Shutt, ST10 3AW, GR 0333438

DISTANCE 2¼ miles (3.6km)

SUMMARY Easy/Moderate with a steep section

MAPS OS Landranger 119

WHERE TO EAT AND DRINK Nowhere on route

A walk through part of a woodland nature reserve belonging to the National Trust.

Walk down the road B5147 towards Cheadle to reach The Grange. Opposite, take a footpath that leads across fields and comes out on Dark Lane. Turn left along the lane for ¼ mile to reach a stile on the right.

1️⃣ Go over and then through a pedestrian gate and down through fields towards woodland. It can be very muddy after rain. Proceed down, keeping Gibridding Wood on your left, and follow round sharp right, then left, and continue downwards and through a kissing gate.

2️⃣ Go left into a gully, and General Martin's Stone can be seen to the right within a stock-proof fence on a hillock; continue downwards with woodland still on your left, and over stiles to pass a small lake on the left before reaching East Wall Farm.

3️⃣ Do not go over the stile in front of the farm, but go right and around the farm; shortly afterwards turn left along a track to go into the woodlands of Hawksmoor Nature Reserve.

4️⃣ Shortly after entering the woodlands the track forks; take the right fork and soon on the right take a footpath marked by waymarks on small posts. This ascends steeply and can be followed back to the B5417 and car park.

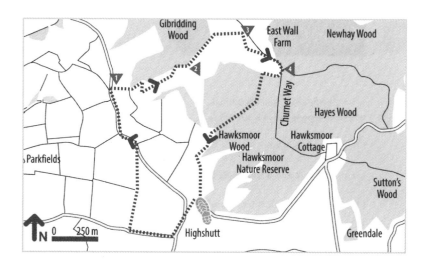

Points of interest

General Martin's Stone was erected to the memory of General William Reid Martin who died on this spot following a fall from his horse on 31 December 1892.

Hawksmoor Nature Reserve is a fine reserve created during the late 1920s at the suggestion of J. R. B. Masefield. A plaque at the main entrance gate records his keen interest and great love for the natural history of the area.

Ecton Copper Mines

START The Peak District car park at Hulme End, SK17 0EZ, GR 103593

DISTANCE 3 miles (5km)

SUMMARY Short with a steep section

MAPS OS Landranger 119

WHERE TO EAT AND DRINK The Manifold Inn, Hulme End, Hartington T01298 84537; Hulme End Tea Junction T01298 687368

Pleasant family walk skirting early industrial remains.

① Leave the car park along the surfaced Manifold Trail for about 150m, then go left over a stile and diagonally right across a field to another stile in the boundary fence. Head in a similar direction to a footbridge over the river. Cross the footbridge to a road and farm. Go right along the road for about 300m, following the river, then turn left by the cottage.

② Follow the lane past a fishpond and boathouse where the road bends sharply right and uphill. After 100m go right up a lane that contours the hillside, rising gradually to a squeezer by old mine shafts.

③ Go through the squeezer and follow the field boundary down the hill to a stile in a wall by some buildings. The landslip on your left is a result of ancient mining. Go over the stile and turn right down the lane past a Gothic building, and down to the road. At the road pick up the Manifold Trail again, which will take you back to the car park.

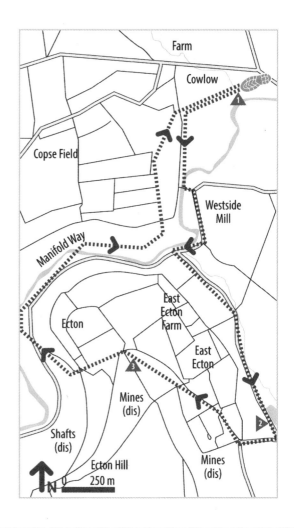

Cowlow

Copse Field

Westside
Mill

Manifold Way

East
Ecton
Farm

Ecton

East
Ecton

Mines
(dis)

Shafts
(dis)

Ecton Hill

Mines
(dis)

0   250 m
N

Points of interest

Mine shafts – some mine shafts are inadequately fenced, so
great care must be taken. The shafts are part of the derelict Ecton
mines, closed in 1873; they were once the largest in Europe.

6

7

Hollington Level

START At the parking area next to the junction of the Cheadle to Hollington road, GR 036398

DISTANCE 3½ miles (5.5km)

SUMMARY Easy

MAPS OS Landranger 128

WHERE TO EAT AND DRINK The Raddle Inn, ¼ mile up the Hollington lane from Great Gate, www.raddleinn. com (T01889 507 278)

A walk over fields and country lanes.

① Across the road from the parking area a stile leads into a field. In the distance can be seen the Weaver Hills, which form the southern part of the Pennine chain. Walk down the field and emerge on to the Winnoth Dale to Great Gate road, and turn right along it towards Great Gate. In spring and summer lovely birdsong may be heard in the woodland to the left of this lane.

② About ½ mile further on, Locker's Lane joins it from the right, but you keep straight ahead and soon come to the small village of Great Gate. On entering the village, turn right and proceed up the hill towards Hollington.

③ At the first sharp corner take a public footpath that goes off right into a field; it follows a winding track and eventually reaches the road at the west end of Hollington village. Turn right along the road to reach the parking area at the start. This section is known as Hollington Level, and the Weaver Hills again come into view to the right. On the opposite side and much further away, The Wrekin in Shropshire and the hills in Wales can be seen in exceptionally clear weather.

A short version of the walk can be taken, by following the route to ②. Where Locker's Lane joins it from the right, about ½ mile further on, turn up this lane to reach the Hollington to Cheadle road near Paradise Cottage. Turn right along the road to reach the parking area at the start, and the Weaver Hills again come into view to the

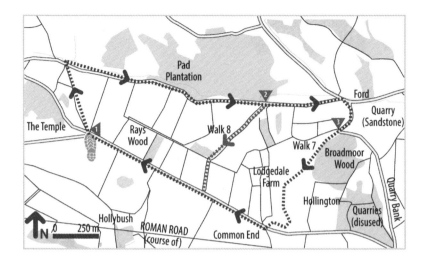

right. On the opposite side and much further away The Wrekin in Shropshire and hills in Wales can be seen in exceptionally clear weather.

Great Gate: It is said that the name comes from it having been the 'Great Gate' or main gateway to Croxden Abbey, situated to the south; the abbey is now a ruin, cared for by English Heritage.

High Shutt

START Inside the entrance to Hawksmoor Nature Reserve, ST10 3AW, GR 039443

DISTANCE 3 miles (5km) or 5 miles (8km)

SUMMARY Easy/Moderate

MAPS OS Landranger 119

WHERE TO EAT AND DRINK Nowhere on route

A fine walk through this National Trust nature reserve.

Cross over the B5417 and go down Green Dale lane for a little over ¼ mile, passing cottages on the left. Shortly afterwards go over a stile on the right which leads into fields, and pick up a farm track following a wall up to Highshutt Farm. The path goes through the farmyard and emerges on to a lane; here, turn right up a track and follow it for ¼ mile to reach the B5417. Turn left along the road for 120yd and take a path in the right corner of the layby to enter Hawksmoor Nature Reserve.

① Once in the reserve, take the path to the left, which eventually leads down to a track. Off to the left is a junction of tracks.

② Turn along the right branch, and follow this through woodlands all the way until it reaches the B5417, where you turn right along the road to return to the start.

A very fine, longer walk can be made by continuing Walk 4 with this walk. From Highshutt Farm go right out of the farmyard, but instead of taking the track to the right, go down the minor road to the B5417, and turn left down to The Grange.

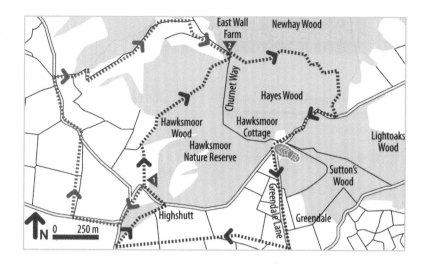

Points of interest

Hawksmoor Nature Reserve is a fine reserve created during the late 1920s at the suggestion of J. R. B. Masefield. A plaque at the main entrance gate records his keen interest and great love for the natural history of the area.

10 Great Gate and Bradley

START The small parking area at the triangular junction, S10 4HE, GR 053400

DISTANCE 3½ miles (5.5km)

SUMMARY Easy

MAPS OS Landranger 128

WHERE TO EAT AND DRINK The Raddle Inn, ¼ mile up the Hollington lane from Great Gate, www.raddleinn. com (T01889 507 278)

A walk over fields and country roads, taking in the ruins of an abbey.

1 Walk over the footbridge beside the ford, and go through the village in the direction of Alton. At the far end of the village, where the road to Croxden and Rocester goes off to the right, there is a stone stile in the wall on the left. Go over this and walk up the fields towards Bradley; the route eventually crosses the farm track that goes up to Wood Farm. Just beyond this the path passes a bungalow, from where the hamlet and church of Bradley come into view ahead. The way leads down the field, across a stream and up the fields to Bradley.

2 On reaching the lane at Bradley, turn right. Go right again at the junction, back in the direction of Great Gate.

3 Not far along this lane there is a stone stile on the left in a section of holly hedge. Cross this into the field, and keep to the ditch on your right. At the bottom cross the footbridge and walk about 30yd up to the corner of the hedge ahead. Go over the stile into the next field and walk up the field with the hedge on your right. At the top of this field is a ridge of ground from where, tradition has it, Cromwell's cannons were fired at during the Civil War. As you go down the field the ruins of the abbey lie ahead.

4 The ruins are on private land but are open to the public: if you wish to visit them, turn left along the road, and retrace your steps afterwards; if you do not, turn right along the road back to Great Gate, and return through the village to the parking area at the start.

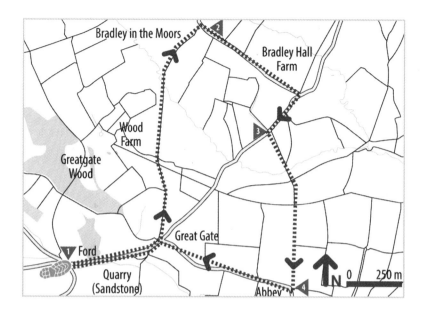

Points of interest

 The name 'Great Gate' is said to derive from the fact that it was the main gateway to Croxden Abbey, situated to the south (*see* below).

Bradley church was built in 1750 and stands on the site of an earlier church. In the churchyard is the tomb of Anne Snape, who is said to have died of a broken heart. The inscription on the stone records that her death broke a true lovers' knot, and that she died as long ago as 25 March 1307.

Croxden Abbey dates from 1174 and was occupied by Cistercian monks. The ruins are in the care of English Heritage and are on private land, but are always open to the public.

Harston Wood and Foxt

START The picnic site at the old Froghall Wharf, ST10 2HJ, GR 026476

DISTANCE 3½ miles (5.5km)

SUMMARY Easy, but with some steep sections

MAPS OS Landranger 119

WHERE TO EAT AND DRINK Nothing on route

An easy walk through woods and fields with a few steep sections, sometimes following the old railway track.

1 From the picnic site, walk up the track of the dismantled railway for about ¾ mile. The gradient here is gradual, and on the way you pass the tall, natural column of sandstone called Harston Rock situated on the right, in Harston Wood.

2 About ¼ mile after passing the rock the route leaves the rail track and branches to the right, going through woodland, with a stream on the left. Eventually the path curves round to the left into fields, then returns to the railway track again. On reaching it, turn left.

3 When you come to the stone bridge that passes over the track, walk underneath the bridge and then immediately up the embankment and over the stile by the bridge. The route now crosses the bridge in the direction of Foxt. Go over and down fields, and cross Shirley Brook by the footbridge. Beyond, the route climbs steeply upwards: take the old track between stone walls to Foxt. In the village, turn left towards Froghall; after ⅓ mile you will pass a row of cottages on the left. Turn left past the end of the cottages, and go steeply down fields to cross Shirley Brook again at another footbridge. Our route climbs gradually up through the wood to rejoin the old railway track. Go right to return to the starting point.

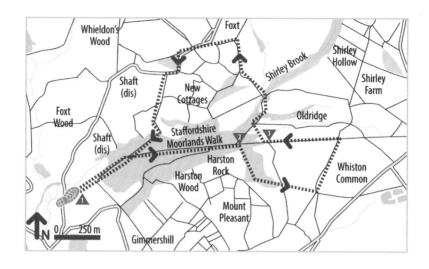

Points of interest

The dismantled railway/tramway was built in 1777 to enable horse-drawn traffic to haul limestone down to Froghall from the high ground at Cauldon. It was conveyed away from Froghall by canal.

12 Flash and Dun Cow's Grove

START **The layby near the Travellers Rest Inn on the A53, SK17 0SN, GR 032678**

DISTANCE **3¾ miles (6km)**

SUMMARY **Fairly easy**

MAPS **OS Landranger 119 Explorer OL24**

WHERE TO EAT AND DRINK **There are three eating places at Quarnford, near Buxton: the Flash Car Stores Café on the A53, www.maccinfo. com/Flash/Index.html (T01298 22763), open Mon–Tues 8am–5.30pm, Wed–Fri 8am–6pm, Sat–Sun 8.30am–5pm; The Travellers Rest, www.theknightstable.co.uk/ (T01298 23695), closed Mons and Tues except Bank Holidays; and The New Inn (T01298 22941)**

A fairly easy walk with good views of millstone grit hills and valleys.

☐1 From the layby take the main road north for a short way and then turn first left. Soon after a road junction to the right, pass the farm at Oxensitch on the left and, immediately beyond, cross a stile on the left. Follow the path ahead uphill, keeping to the right of a hollow and a fence, and gradually bearing right from them. At the right-angle of the fence, go over a stile (which can be easily missed) and take the left fork of two paths. Follow this diagonally across the field towards a wall which should be crossed. Continue straight on, with the wall on the right, as the path becomes a track which bends to the left into Flash.

☐2 At the road junction turn left, pass The New Inn, and cross straight over at the next junction, following a signposted path down the right-hand side of the church. This turns left through a gate and into a farmyard, where you go right: follow a track through to a second gate and metal stile. Go through, and follow a similar line over more stiles and across fields until you reach the main road. Cross this and take the track almost opposite. Shortly afterwards, bear left when the track forks, and pass a farm to cross a stile on the left, noting the direction of the yellow waymarker. Proceed in this direction across open access land to reach a stile in the corner at

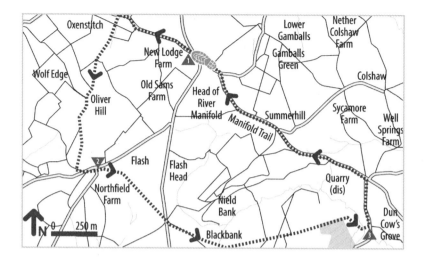

the top where two walls meet. Continue on the left of a wall, then a fence, then another wall, walking to the left of Brand Plantation; cross a stile on the right shortly afterwards. The route leads down to Dun Cow's Grove.

3️⃣ Here, cross the infant River Manifold and join the road. Turn left on the road and up the hill to a road junction. Turn left, and continue up the hill back to the start point.

Points of interest

At 1,518ft above sea level, Flash is the highest village in England. It gave its name to the slang term for counterfeit money, because in the past, 'coiners' had their headquarters here.

The Dove and Manifold Valleys

START The car park in Longnor Market, SK17 0NT, GR 088649

DISTANCE 4 miles (6.5km)

SUMMARY Fairly easy, with a long, moderately steep incline

MAPS OS Landranger 119

WHERE TO EAT AND DRINK Ye Old Cheshire Cheese, High Street, Longnor, www.cheshirecheeselongnor.co.uk (T01298 83218). The Pack Horse Inn, Crowdecote, www.thepack-horseinn.co.uk (T01298 83618), open for food midday until 2.30pm and evening until 9pm, Wed–Sun. Cobbles Café, Market Place, Longnor, www.cobblescafe.co.uk/ (T01298 83166), open usually Thurs–Sun 8.30am–4pm

A short and very scenic tour of the two famous Peak District valleys; it can be muddy in places.

1️⃣ Go east out of the village until you reach the speed-limit signs. Here, turn left down a lane and bear right after 200yd to head downhill to a barn. Go left of the barn and immediately right, and follow the bridlepath across fields to the River Dove. Go over the footbridge and continue for about 150yd.

2️⃣ Turn right over a stile, and continue to the hamlet of Crowdecote. Take the road right, passing the Packhorse Inn, and then turn left down a lane for 150yd. At this point go right down a short lane, and cross the River Dove by the footbridge.

3️⃣ Turn left to Under Whittle; in the second field the path swings up and away from the river to a stile, which you cross. Go up a small bank to another stile in a post and wire fence. Cross this, and head up to the top right corner and across another stile; follow a path towards two stone barns. Just before the barns, take the wooden stile on the right over a post and wire fence, and veer left uphill to a stile in the corner. Cross this, and follow the path passing Upper and Under Whittle Farms; join a lane heading upwards, until you meet a road.

④ Turn right for ⅓ mile to a left turn; go down this lane for about 200yd and through a gate on the right to head down the field along a track that 'S-bends' down to a farm. Follow the arrows straight through the farmyard, leaving it by a made-up track. In about 100yd you come to a stile set in the middle of nowhere.

⑤ Cross this, heading right, and follow the squeezers along the banks of the River Manifold towards Longnor. Finally head up the slope towards a farm and the village. At the road turn left, to regain the marketplace.

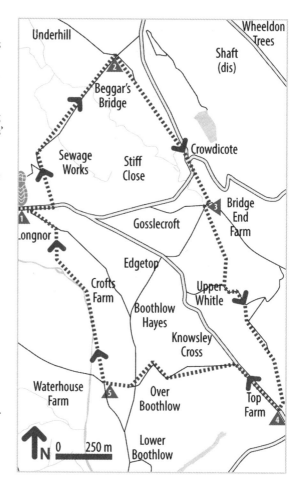

Points of interest

The River Dove – this famous river forms the boundary between Staffordshire and Derbyshire, and between gritstone and limestone country.

14 Wootton and the Weaver Hills

Start In Back Lane, Wootton DE6 2GW, GR 105452

Distance 4 miles (6.5km)

Summary The uphill section can be strenuous

Maps OS Landranger 119

Where to eat and drink There are no convenient venues

A steady climb to a hilltop is rewarded by beautiful and far-ranging views.

1 Take the Leek road, and just after Show Croft Farm, turn right on a rough track (Gidacre Lane). Where the track ends, a gate leads into the cricket ground on the left.

2 Cross the wooden stile in the corner of the hedge, and cross the field to the diagonally opposite corner where there are double wooden gates. Go through, cross the next field to the far left wall and into the next field. Head up to the diagonally opposite corner and over a stile. Continue upwards to the left, and round the hillside to a stile; after this the route levels out and follows round a wall corner. Cross more stiles to the summit over on the left – the approach is clearly marked. The views from here are extensive. Retrace your steps from the summit back into the field, and follow the right edge to a stile.

3 Go through to a reasonably clear path and along the left field boundary. Proceed in this direction across fields to an unfenced lane. Go right and descend the lane, passing the humps and hollows of Raddle Pits workings to a 90-degree bend.

4 Go straight ahead across the stile and down the field to a corner stile and Hall Lane. Go right and follow the lane back to the start.

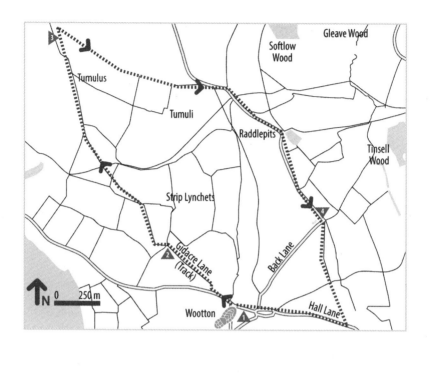

Points of interest

Raddle Pits is a working mine that is still used for the extraction of
red ochre, a substance used as a colouring pigment.

15 Ramblers Retreat to Oldfurnace

START **The Ramblers Retreat Café,** ST10 4BU, GR 062432

DISTANCE **4 miles (6.5km)**

SUMMARY **Moderate**

MAPS **OS Landranger 128**

WHERE TO EAT AND DRINK **The Ramblers Retreat (T01538 702730).www. ramblersretreat.co.uk: Mar–Oct Mon–Fri 10am–5pm, weekends 10am–6pm; Nov–Feb Mon–Fri 10.30am–3pm, weekends 10am–5pm**

This lovely walk goes through woodland and has impressive views of the local valleys.

1 Facing the front of the café, take the path signposted Woodland Walk that veers off to the right: you will reach a gradually ascending sandstone track with woods on its right. Pass an old smelting mill, a fishpond and a small lake, all on the left. Keep to the right of Earls Rock and continue following the track upwards until eventually you come to a track, partly tarmac and with a cattlegrid just to the right.

2 Turn left away from the cattlegrid and follow the track, passing the Youth Hostel and to the right of a small building. Follow the stone wall on the right. There are fine views of the valley below from here. Cross the memorial stile and follow the path down through the trees to more fishponds.

3 Turn right and follow the path, soon with a stream on your left; go for almost a mile to Oldfurnace.

4 Turn left on the road, and after about 50yd go over the style next to a farm gate on the left. Go diagonally right uphill, keeping to the left of a gully until you reach a fence. Follow the fronts along the left, to a stile. Cross over a stile on to Carriage Drive, a wide track, and go left along it for a few hundred yards until it curves left.

5 Here, take the ascending path on the right, and follow it to a stile at the top; cross the stile into a field, and go straight over the field to the

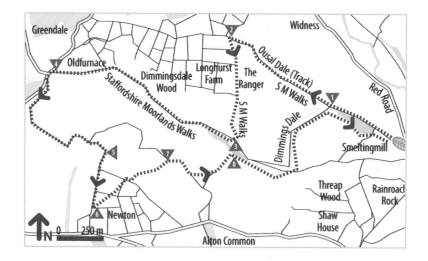

corner of a coppice, where you join a farm track. Turn right along this track; there are fine views over the Staffordshire Dales.

6 Just before reaching a cottage situated on the right, go over a stile on the left next to the corner of a stone wall; go over this into a field, and take a path which almost comes back on yourself. Cross the field diagonally to another stile. Cross this stile into a second field, and cross to another, clearly visible stile. In the third field turn right along the wall to a stile in a corner. Cross into a fourth, large field and go diagonally across it, passing to the right of a large oak tree. Go down to a stile in the right corner, by woods.

7 Cross into a fifth field, keeping to the right edge until you reach a stile. Cross into woods; in a few yards keep to the right, following a gradually descending path. At a fork bear left, going more steeply down to reach Carriage Drive again.

8 Turn right to follow this wide track back to the Ramblers Retreat where the walk started.

Hulme End and Brund

16

Start **The Hulme End car park, SK17 0EZ, GR 102594**

Distance **4 miles (6.5km)**

Summary **Easy**

Maps **OS Landranger 119 Explorer OL24**

Where to eat and drink **At Hulme End there is The Manifold Inn, www.themanifoldinn.co.uk/ default.html, (T01298 84537); and also The Tea Junction, www. teajunctionhulmeend.co.uk, (T01298 687368)**

An easy walk, mainly along minor roads.

1 From the car park entrance go along the B5054 through Hulme End village, over the River Manifold and up a short steep hill on the other side. As the incline levels out, take the minor road on the left signposted to Sheen and Longnor. Follow this downhill, go over a stream, and then up the slope on the other side.

2 Soon afterwards, turn left on to the track to Low End Farm. Follow the track through the farmyard, and soon afterwards pass through a gate and continue straight on. The path peters out, but head virtually straight onwards, aiming for the right-hand end of the line of trees, keeping a wall on the left. Negotiate another gate, then continue straight on, keeping to the right of a stream that runs off to the left. Pass through a wall, then through two gates in quick succession on to a track, and join a minor road. Turn left along this, passing through Brund, and continue to a road junction.

3 Turn left here, signposted to Hulme End, pass Brund Mill, and cross the bridge over the River Manifold. Continue until a road junction, where you turn left. At another road junction nearly a mile ahead, again turn left, and continue until you reach the B5054. Here turn right, and shortly afterwards on the left is the car park where you started.

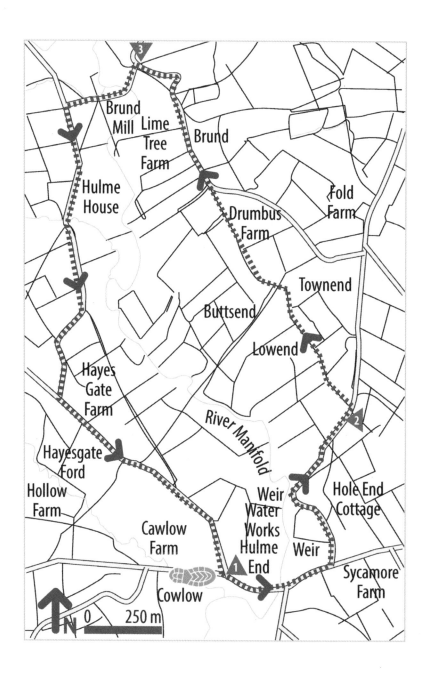

Brund
Mill
Lime
Tree
Farm

Brund

Hulme
House

Drumbus
Farm

Fold
Farm

Townend

Buttsend

Lowend

Hayes
Gate
Farm

River Manifold

Hayesgate
Ford

Hollow
Farm

Weir
Water
Works
Hulme
End

Hole End
Cottage

Cawlow
Farm

Weir

Cowlow

Sycamore
Farm

N   0   250 m

The Manifold Trail

Start The public car park in Wetton, DE6 2AF, GR 108552

Distance 4 miles (6.5km)

Summary Some steep ascents and descents, but also some level sections

Maps OS Landranger 119, Explorer OL24

Where to eat and drink The Royal Oak, Wetton, www.royaloakwetton.co.uk, (T01335 310287): Mon and Tues closed, Wed–Sun 12:00–23:00

A relatively easy introduction to the hills and dales found in the Staffordshire area of the Peak National Park.

1. Turn right from the car park, then right again along the lane, and left at the T-junction. After a few yards turn left over a wall stile. Follow the clear path across fields; it descends steeply, passing signed footpaths to Thor's Cave, to reach the Manifold Trail across a footbridge. The river bed may be dry, as for most part of the year the river runs underground.

2. Turn right along the Trail for an easy and scenically beautiful walk to the junction with the road from Wetton, to the right. Leave the Trail to go straight ahead over a stile into a little valley.

3. Here, the path follows a stream to a wall stile adjacent to a stone building. Go over the stile and cross a footbridge, then veer left to follow the contour round the lower level of the hill to its far side.

4. The path picks up a boundary wall at a field corner, and follows this for approximately 300 yards before turning left through a stile. After this, turn right along a clear, stiled path across fields and past old stone barns to reach Wetton at the village street adjacent to a farmhouse. Go down the street and past the pub, turning first right back to the car park.

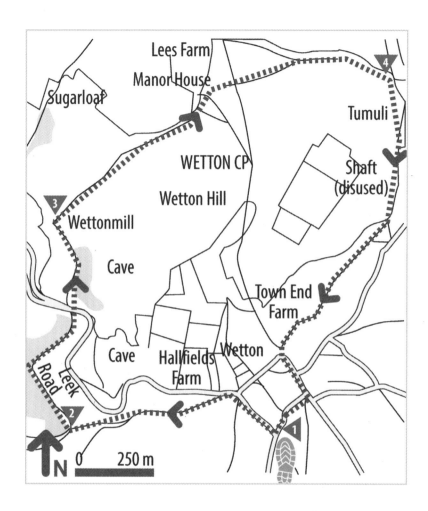

Lees Farm
Manor House
Sugarloaf
Tumuli
WETTON CP
Shaft
(disused)
Wetton Hill
Wettonmill
Cave
Town End
Farm
Cave
Wetton
Hallfields
Farm
Leek Road
N 0 250 m

Points of interest

The Manifold Trail runs along the bed of the defunct Leek and Manifold Light Railway, which operated between Waterhouses and Hulme End.

18 Castle Ring

START The car park at Castle Ring, WS15 4QZ, GR 045126

DISTANCE 4 miles (6.5km)

SUMMARY Easy, but with a steep climb towards the end

MAPS OS Landranger 128

WHERE TO EAT AND DRINK Park Gate Inn, in Park Gate Road, Cannock Wood, www.theparkgatepub.com, (T01543 682223)

A fine walk in Cannock Chase, an Area of Outstanding Natural Beauty.

1 From the car park, face the information board about the hill fort, and go left on to a path waymarked The Heart of England Way. Follow this well waymarked path into the forest fringe and down a forest ride that bends slightly left before joining another track; go right and down into a valley and up the other side where eventually you come to a road, just over 1 mile from Castle Ring.

2 Before the road, veer right along a path that runs almost parallel with the road, before shortly reaching a forest track. Turn right, and go down the valley to a large pool on the right; ahead is a junction of forest roads.

3 Turn right and continue, ignoring a branch going left. Now follows a pleasant walk through mostly coniferous woodland until you reach a forester's track cut through the trees on the left. Continue past this, and after 50yd you will drop into a dip with a culverted stream. Go a further 50yd and there is another track on the left, but ignore this: keep going for another 50yd and again ignore a track on the left. 100yd further there is a track on the right: ignore this, too.

4 But a further 50yd ahead there is a grassy track on the left, turning back sharply: take this, and start to ascend. This path emerges on to a forest track. Go left to a turning ahead, where the track finishes. Just beyond this take a path on the right, and climb upwards to reach the ramparts of Castle Ring hill fort – and so back to the car park.

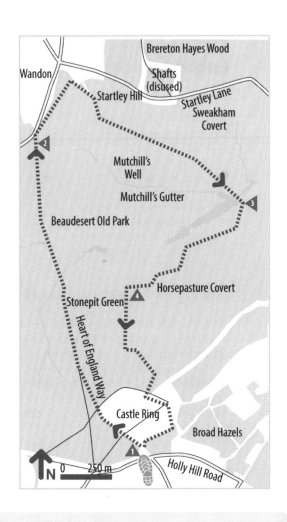

Points of interest

🔍 Castle Ring hill fort was built around 500BC; it is a well preserved example covering 9 acres and comprising several ramparts and ditches. The site includes the remains of a much later building, thought to be a mediaeval hunting lodge associated with the Royal Forest of Cannock Chase.

19 Ipstones and Consallgforge

START On the road west from the centre of Ipstones village, ST10 2LA, GR 105497

DISTANCE 4 miles (6.5km)

SUMMARY A steep descent through trees and a steeply ascending stepped path, but otherwise fairly easy, including a level section along a canal towpath

MAPS OS Landranger 119

WHERE TO EAT AND DRINK The Marquis of Granby in Church Lane, Ipstones (no website, T01538 266462); phone for opening times

A fairly easy walk through some beautiful woodlands.

1 Walk a short distance along the road away from Ipstones, and take a path left over fields towards Booths Wood Farm. As you approach the farm go over a stile on the left, turn left and down to another stile; beyond this the route goes into woods and down an engineered path to a footbridge. Cross this and a stile, and climb upwards to meet a trackway which takes you out of the wood. Veer left up to the corner of the field boundary, and keeping this on your left, follow it to the next field.

2 Almost halfway along, turn right down to a stile, and enter the top of the woods. Follow the path as it winds its way steeply downwards out of the woods to reach the canal and Cherryeye Bridge.

3 Cross the bridge and follow the towpath to the right all the way to the Black Lion pub at Consallforge.

4 Leave the canal here, and walk past the front of the pub, turning right and then left after the building to take a path up the side of the valley through a wood. Ascend the many steps of the Devil's Staircase, and carry straight on to a stile just past a large dip on the right. Cross the stile and turn right at the road ahead. Shortly

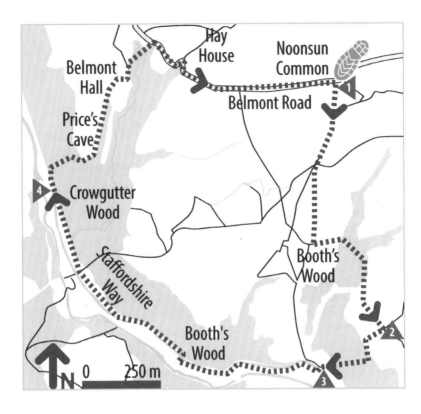

afterwards, turn right on to a footpath and descend the steps. At the bottom, follow the path on the left-hand side of a stream, then cross the stream and follow the path up to a road. Turn right on this, and follow it back to the start of the walk.

Points of interest

There are some delightful bluebell woods en route, especially on the far bank from the towpath of the canal.

Froghall Wharf and Harston Wood

START The picnic site at the old Froghall Wharf, ST10 2HJ, GR 026476

DISTANCE 4 miles (6.5km)

SUMMARY Moderate

MAPS OS Landranger 119

WHERE TO EAT AND DRINK Fox and Goose, at Foxt (T01538 266415); phone for opening times

A delightful wooded walk through our early industrial past, past fascinating rock formations; there is always a good show of spring flowers.

① Go over the canal bridge, then turn left and down on to the Cauldon Canal bank. After passing cottages on the right, drop down again to a footbridge: go over this and up the other side. Turn right along a track into Moseymoor Wood, following Blackbank Brook. The path steepens.

② Take a right fork down to the head of an old reservoir dam and keep to the right at the next fork. Continue along the obvious track upwards, with the brook on your right. Cross another well made footbridge, and go up the bank through Whieldon's Wood. Leave the wood at a squeezer and stile, and head across fields. Turn right through a gate, and then immediately left across fields to a lane and Foxt village. Go straight over the road along the tarmac lane past a farm stop. Continue to a narrow walled lane in a wood, which runs downwards to meet another footpath. Go left and over a stile, and follow another walled lane upwards to where it flattens out and joins a footpath.

③ Turn left, and follow this path to the diagonally opposite corner of the field, and continue in a more or less similar line through a series of tall holly hedges. The path zigzags a little and bears right, eventually reaching a lane beside a farm.

④ Take a path through the gate on your right and down to Newfields Gallery. Pass this building and go into a field, where you

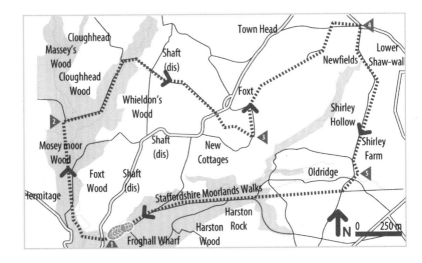

drop down over a steep bank; there is a stile in the bottom with a footbridge beyond. Go over these, and follow the route which goes across fields to the right of Shirley Farm to Oldridge, leaving a large rock behind you.

⑤ Go up the bank to reach the old tramway. Turn right along the tramway and follow it back to the car park.

Points of interest

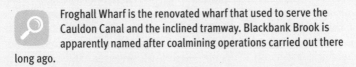

Froghall Wharf is the renovated wharf that used to serve the Cauldon Canal and the inclined tramway. Blackbank Brook is apparently named after coalmining operations carried out there long ago.

The old tramway worked on a pulley system, where the weight of the loaded trucks full of limestone running downhill pulled the empty trucks up the incline to the top. The tramway served Cauldon quarries.

Oakamoor, Farley and Churnet Valley

START **The Oakamoor Picnic site, ST10 2DQ, GR 053448**

DISTANCE **4 miles (6.5km)**

SUMMARY **Moderate**

MAPS **OS Landranger 119**

WHERE TO EAT AND DRINK **The Ramblers Retreat café. (Turn left out of the car park and go down the lane for 1½ miles)**

A walk with fine views over the Churnet Valley and the Farley and Wootton estates.

① From the picnic site, go across the footbridge and turn right. Go to a log bar, then veer left to a kissing gate near the end of one of the old railway platforms. Go through the kissing gate into a field, and walk uphill along the hedge on the left. At the top go through a hedge gap into a field, and continue straight ahead. Cross a farm track and veer right to go through a gate/over a stile into a field. Go round a low iron railing to a stone wall on the left, and follow it along to a stile, and so on to the road. Turn right and go to a T-junction in Farley. Turn right, cross the road, and go left up the lane between stone houses to a stile at its end. Cross the stile and follow the path to the left (not the path straight ahead going downhill). Watch out for herds of deer from here on.

② Follow the fence to a stile, and continue along the fence until the remnants of a stone wall are seen down the slope; carry on down so you are on the right of the wall. Keep going until you see a stile in the fence ahead: cross this into a field. Keep to the right of a fence, and head for a tree on a hillock. Go towards the white farmhouse; shortly you will also see a derelict cottage on the right. Go round the back of the cottage, and cross a field to a ladder stile, which you cross into the next field. Go across the field to a stile situated on the right of a farmhouse.

③ Cross on to Longshaw Lane, and turn left along it to Ramshorn Road. Turn left along the road to a crossroads, where you turn left on to Beelow Lane; shortly after turn right on to a wide path, and follow

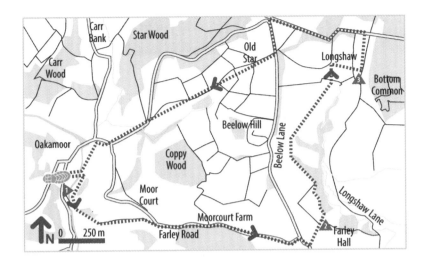

this downhill. Cross over a stile in the right corner, into a field. Keep left, and go downhill through two fields to reach a farm track. Cross the track to a stile, and go over this into a field. Veer over to the left to a gap in the hedge. Go through the gap, and still going downhill, continue until you get to a stile at the bottom. Cross the stile on to a road and turn left, downhill, to Oakamoor. Turn off left just before the river bridge on to a footpath: this will take you back to the car park.

Longnor and Hollingsclough

START In Longnor village, SK17 0NT, GR 088649. Cars may be parked in the square or on the main road

DISTANCE 4½ miles (7km)

SUMMARY Easy

MAPS OS Landranger 110

WHERE TO EAT AND DRINK In Longnor, Ye Olde Cheshire Cheese, in High Street, www. cheshirecheeselongnor.co.uk (T01298 83218). Also Cobbles Tea Room and Café in the market square, www.cobblescafe.co.uk, Thurs–Sun 8.30am–4pm, but openings seasonal

A fairly easy walk with spectacular scenery.

[1] With the market square on your right, set off over the crossroads. Shortly after, bear right along a minor road (not down the hill); on approaching the farm at Gauledge, take the footpath left. Continue, keeping the wall here immediately on your right. Where the wall ends, head straight across the middle of the next field and over the stile on to a road. Turn left, walking downhill, and turn right after crossing the stream, signposted to Hollingsclough.

[2] In Hollingsclough, turn right at the road junction and after ¼ mile, take the track to the left just before a right-hand bend. Cross over the cattlegrid and follow the track towards Chrome Hill. After ¼ mile take the right fork, and cross the footbridge over the River Dove.

[3] On reaching the road at Stannery – close to Parkhouse Hill – turn right. Almost immediately cross over the stile in the wall on the right, and make for the right-angle of the wall to the left. Walk to the footbridge ahead, and climb partway up Nabend Hill, veering left of the summit through a line of bushes towards the house at Near Nabend. Go over two stiles on the footpath, joining a track that leads to the B5053. Turn right on to the road up the hill, past a house at Highacres, and almost immediately afterwards, take the track left down the hill. Pass to the right of the second of two houses ahead, and cross over the stile on the right. Head up the hill immediately

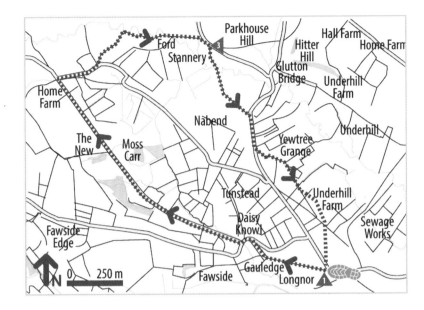

to the right of the house, and on reaching another track, turn left, walking downhill again. At the entrance to the next farm, take the footpath right, up the hill, passing over the stile in the wall at the top. Longnor village can now be seen ahead. Continue on the footpath, keeping to the right of a wall and aiming slightly to the right of the church. At the junction with the road at Lanehead, turn left, cross Church Street, and turn left down the main road. Shortly afterwards, turn left, back into the square at Longnor.

Points of interest

Chrome Hill and Parkhouse Hill – on the walk there are impressive views of these two spectacular limestone peaks, known locally as 'the Dragon's Back'.

23 Three Shires Head

START In the layby near the Travellers Rest Inn, SK17 0SN, GR 032678

DISTANCE 4½ miles (7km)

SUMMARY Easy/moderate

MAPS OS Landranger 119 Explorer OL24

WHERE TO EAT AND DRINK The Travellers Rest at Quarnford, near Buxton, www.theknightstable.co.uk (T01298 23695), closed Mon, Tues, except Bank Holidays

A pleasant all-year-round walk along ancient trails and through Sites of Special Scientific Interest.

⊡ Walk towards Buxton for 500yd, and then go left along a minor road. After 100yd turn right along another minor road. After 300yd, just before a farm, go left over a stile by a gate and along an old green lane between gritstone walls. There are good views from here across Cheshire. Follow the made-up track round to the left to a gate. Continue onwards to a farm: go left in front of it, and down through a gate. Keeping below the gritstone edge, cross the wall to the left, through another gate, and walk past the front of another farm. Keep going along a track to yet another farm, and walk past the front of this one, too; soon you will join a road to reach a T-junction.

② Turn right, and follow the road along; go through a gate and continue to a right-hand bend, then cut down left along a wall for 100yd to reach another made-up road. Turn left through a gate, and go down the valley past a spring; here a stream comes in from the packhorse trail.

③ On arriving at the packhorse bridge at Three Shires Head, turn left towards the River Dane. Follow the track past Panniers Pool, an excellent spot for a picnic and a dip in the summer. Keep to the sandy track that climbs up from the river and valley bottom. Stay on this path, passing several farms. Most of the land to the left and right here was designated a 'Site of Special Scientific Interest' in 1989. Eventually you reach a made-up road: continue left along this; soon

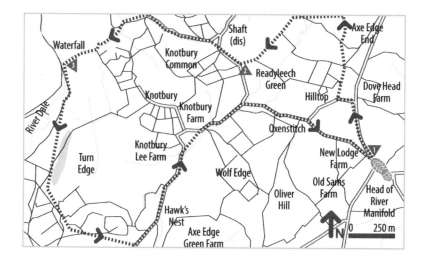

a stream comes in from the right to run parallel with the road. After 500yd the road swings up and left: here go right over a stile, and follow the stream to meet the road again after about 200yd. Follow the road up the hill keeping to the right until you reach the main road and layby.

Points of interest

The packhorse trail on this walk is part of the ancient packhorse trail from the Cheshire plain to Buxton and the industrial Midlands.

The Three Shires Head is situated on the point where Cheshire, Derbyshire and Staffordshire actually meet. In days gone by it was a meeting place for 'flash' counterfeiters because there was easy escape into another county.

Alton and Brookleys Lake

START In Back Lane, Alton ST10 4AN, GR 076424

DISTANCE 4½ miles (7km)

SUMMARY The steep climbs can be strenuous, but other sections of the walk are easy

MAPS OS Landranger 128, or Explorer 259

WHERE TO EAT AND DRINK In Alton there is The Bull's Head in High Street, www.thebullsheadalton. co.uk (T01538 702307); also The Blacksmiths Arms, www. blacksmithsarmsalton.co.uk/ (T01538702111)

This is a good walk for the winter, with one or two steep climbs to keep you warm. It also includes a flavour of two iconic brands, Alton Towers and JCB.

1 Go to the farm at the junction with Castle Hill Road and through the farm gate on the left of Wheel Lane. Go diagonally left across the field to a stile, and down through trees to reach a farm track. Cross the stile opposite, and go through the field beyond; you will come to a bridge over the river. Cross this to reach a path along an old railway. Go over the stile opposite and follow a track. Soon take the steep footpath on the left beside telegraph poles.

2 After some steps, turn right on a wide path and in a few yards turn left on a footpath that crosses a footbridge to enter Alton Towers. Head straight on, following driveways and a paved path past hotels; then past a car-parking area and along a wooden footpath signposted the way you are going into a large parking area. Take the signed footpath left along a tarmac path; in a short distance turn right along a driveway, and right again at the next junction.

3 In a few yards there is a footpath off to the left: take this through shubbery to a stile. Cross the stile to leave Alton Towers, and walk over the field to a second stile. Go across, and downhill to a squeezer stile. Go through, then cross a farm track on to a worn path to reach Wootton

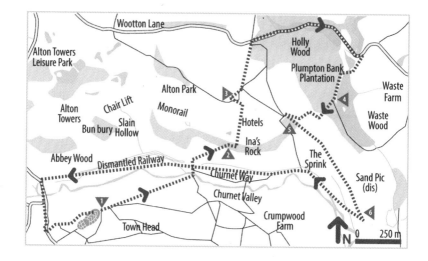

Lane. Turn right and walk for about ¾ mile, passing ponds and streams. Where the road turns sharp left, take a squeezer stile on the right and follow the path, which is waymarked round Brookleys Lake and the JCB test track: the route goes alongside the lake and meets the test track.

4 Here take the waymarked path off to the right, up through woodlands; eventually it crosses a track into a field. Cross the field, still following the waymarkers; the route crosses another track and goes into woods again.

5 In a short distance you come to a fence and a stone stile. Do not go through this, but turn left along a wooded path, keeping the fence and steep drop on your right.

6 At the end the route runs through a narrow fenced section and a metal gate. Here, turn right down a footpath to a track at the bottom. The route goes right, through a gate and past the pumping station at Crumpwood Weir. Beyond the new pumping station follow a surfaced path to join a wide track along the old railway: turn right, and follow this track to Farley Lane at the foot of the valley beneath Alton village. Turn left along the road and up to the village. Turn left up High Street to reach Back Lane.

Rakeway, Freehay and Winnothdale

Start In Rakeway Road, about a mile south-east of Cheadle in a layby ST10 1RA, GR 020420

Distance 4½ miles (7km)

Summary Easy

Maps OS Landranger 119

Where to eat and drink The Queen's at Freehay, www.queensatfreehay. co.uk/index.php (T01538 722383), Mon–Sat 12pm–2pm, 6pm–9.30pm, Sun 12pm–2.30pm, 6.30pm–9.30pm; prices are moderate

A walk through fields and country lanes.

[1] Just to the bottom of the layby, take the track to Rakeway House Farm (B & B), then go left on a path that goes behind Plantation House and over to an unclassified road between Mobberley and Winnothdale, close to an entrance to a quarry. Turn left along the road, and turn right at the second junction. Follow this lane for nearly a mile to an unclassified road and turn right and then next left at crossroads on to the lane towards Great Gate.

[2] Soon a footpath leads off to the left, going up past Spring Farm. Muddy conditions may be encountered at the beginning of this footpath after heavy rain. Follow the path to a lane, and turn left along it. At the roundabout ahead is The Queen's.

[3] Go left at this roundabout, then go straight over the crossroads at Freehay. To avoid walking along the road there is a path on the right that runs parallel with it. About 300yd further on the walk leaves the road by a path to the right. Towards the top of a rise the path goes to the right across a field and then down through woodland to join Rakeway Road. Go left to get back to the start.

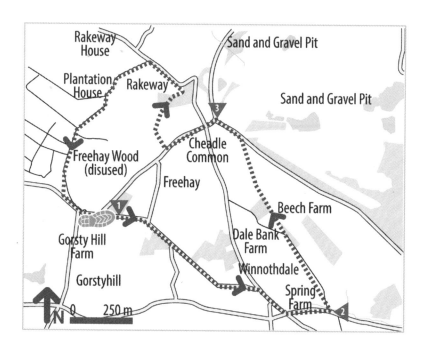

Rakeway House

Sand and Gravel Pit

Plantation House

Rakeway

Sand and Gravel Pit

Freehay Wood (disused)

Cheadle Common

Freehay

Beech Farm

Dale Bank Farm

Gorsty Hill Farm

Winnothdale

Gorstyhill

Spring Farm

0   250 m

N

Tittesworth Reservoir

Start The Visitor Centre, ST13 8SW, GR 993603

Distance 4½ miles (7km)

Summary Easy

Maps OS Landranger 118

Where to eat and drink There is a café that is an integral part of the Visitor Centre (To1538 300180); opening times are seasonal

An interesting walk along good surfaced paths round Tittesworth reservoir.

① Facing the entrance to the Visitor Centre building, walk left (south) along the path, which is well marked by yellow footprint signs. Follow this to reach the River Churnet, and continue until you gain a track through woods; turn off right to cross a stream. Always follow the waymarked route around the inlets of the reservoir, and after a while the reservoir dam wall comes into view. The path rises to meet a track: bear off to the right and down to the dam wall.

② Cross the dam wall and ascend the stepped woodland path; at the top turn right on another path, which looks down on the ancient Hind's Clough Wood. Turn right along the metalled road past North Hillswood Farm to join an unclassified road. Follow this to the right.

③ After a short distance leave the road down a track on the right. When you reach the edge of the reservoir pick up the footpath on the left, which passes the 'Butterfly Beach'. Follow this path: it crosses a couple of footbridges and across pastures to the causeway, where the reservoir is divided; the road runs along the causeway. After crossing the causeway turn right, and you will soon regain the driveway down to the Visitor Centre.

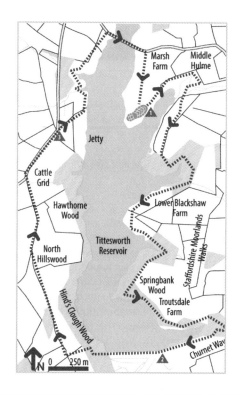

Points of interest

 River Churnet rises in the Western Gritstone Edge, and is the main feeder for the reservoir.

Hind's Clough Wood is an ancient wood of elm, ash, birch, oak, rowan and sycamore. At certain times it provides shelter for red deer.

The dam for the reservoir was constructed between 1959 and 1963; it provides water to the Potteries conurbation.

At the Visitor Centre you can learn how water is stored and delivered, and also about the flora and fauna of the area, which include red deer, badgers, orchids and numerous water-based birds.

Start Wettonmill, where there is off-the-road parking at the bridge, DE6 2AG, GR 095561

Maps OS Landranger 119, Explorer OL24

Distance 4½ miles (7km)

Where to eat and drink The tearooms at Wetton Mill run by National Trust tenants, To1298 84838

Summary Easy

A fairly easy walk with interesting limestone hill and valley scenery.

1 Walk to the crossroads and take the road signposted to Butterton, then bear slightly right in front of the ford and go over a stile on the left along the drystone wall (not through the wooden gate). Cross the footbridge, and follow the path up the hill, forking right and climbing the contours of Ossoms Hill. On the way up the route crosses a stile over a fence, which may be obscured behind a tree. The path beyond climbs upwards, and then continues at approximately the same level, following the bend of the brook below and keeping the wood on the right. The path bends round the hill through fields and across stiles, heading slightly left of a farm, and then joins the track from the farm. Go left along the track, and just past the barn on the right the public footpath turns right into a field. It then turns left halfway into the field, and in the corner of the boundary beyond it rejoins the farm lane. Follow this to the right, and past the church.

2 Here turn left, and then immediately right. As the road forks, bear left and then left again on to the road leading to Wetton. Continue along the road.

3 Immediately after a steep, sharp left-hand bend, there is a path on the right: proceed downhill on this path, crossing a stile in a group of trees at the bottom, on to the Manifold Way track. Turn left along the track, cross the Grindon–Wetton road, and follow the track all the way back to the Wettonmill crossroads. The bed of the river on the right is usually dry in dry weather.

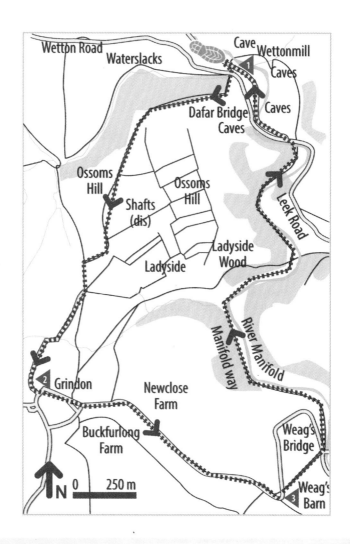

Wetton Road
Waterslacks
Cave
Wettonmill
Caves
Caves
Dafar Bridge
Caves
Ossoms
Hill
Ossoms
Hill
Shafts
(dis)
Leek Road
Ladyside
Wood
Ladyside
Ladyside
Manifold way
River Manifold
Grindon
Newclose
Farm
Weag's
Bridge
Buckfurlong
Farm
Weag's
Barn

N   0   250 m

Points of interest

From Ossoms Hill there are good views across the valley to Ecton Hill and Wetton Hill. In the opposite direction are extensive views to Butterton and the moors beyond.

High Peak Trail

START The Minninglow car park, DE4 2PN, GR 194582

MAPS OS Landranger 119, Exporer OL24

DISTANCE 4½ miles (7km)

SUMMARY Easy

WHERE TO EAT AND DRINK Refreshments are available on the walk at Parwich, Winster or even Hartington

An easy walk, half on a disused railway track, now the High Peak Trail, the other half along old lanes.

1 From the car park take the High Peak Trail, crossing the road that goes to Pikehall. Follow the trail as it goes through a wood and heads for Gotham and the notable Gotham Bend. Continue on the trail for another half mile or so beyond the bend, to where a lane crosses it.

2 This is Green Lane: turn left down it, and in less than a mile you come to a junction of two old ways.

3 Go left along Cobblersnook Lane. After about half a mile the wall on your left disappears, but keep following a wall on the right across a field, and pick up the lane again at the far side. Half a mile further on you come to The Nook, and the lane becomes metalled. Soon after the cottage you cross a minor road; continue in the same direction along Minninglow Lane. A mile or so further on, by a pond on your right, the lane curves left for a few yards, then bends sharply right to meet the High Peak Trail again.

4 Turn left along the trail for a pleasant level walk about a mile back to the car park.

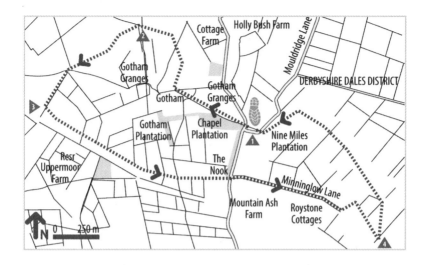

Points of interest

Parts of the High Peak Trail follow the old railway, which was an industrial line that carried lime products. Look over the sides now and then to consider the work entailed in building this line. The lanes on the walk were part of an old packhorse way from Hartington to Wirksworth.

Dilhorne and Tickhill Lane

START The village hall and recreation centre in Dilhorne, ST10 2PQ, GR 971435

DISTANCE 4½ miles (7km)

SUMMARY Easy

MAPS OS Landranger 118

WHERE TO EAT AND DRINK The Royal Oak at Dilhorne, www. royaloakdilhorne.co.uk/index.html for opening times and details

An easy walk across fields, through woodland and along a country lane.

1 Turn right along the road, and after about 100yd take a track on the left signposted 'Footpath'. Pass a pool, and just afterwards cross over a wooden stile on the right near a farm gate. The path crosses fields, using stiles, towards a wood. Pass through the wood and cross over the railway into the woodland at the other side.

2 The path through this section of woodland can be indistinct, but after a small footbridge it generally follows a post and wire fence on the left as it curves right and then left until it comes out into a field. Proceed up the field, sweeping round to the right to a track between stone walls. Bear left towards Newhill Farm, beyond which the walk reaches Tickhill Lane.

3 Turn left along the lane for nearly a mile until you come to a wooden stile on the left (near a gate).

4 Cross this, and go across fields and through a small plantation to reach a surfaced track up to a farm. On reaching the farm itself do not enter the yard, but go through gate on the left and across the field, keeping the farm on your right. Having left the farm behind, continue along the field with the hedge on your right for a short distance, then go straight ahead and down to cross the railway. Very shortly the path crosses an old bridge over a small stream; after a stile take the left path as directed, to go up the field ahead. After crossing two more stiles, veer right across the next field.

5 At its far boundary you will come to a stile next to a gate: go over the stile to join a farm track. Continue along the track through gateways/ stiles, passing the farm on the right, and join the road in the village of Dilhorne. Turn left to reach the recreation centre and car park.

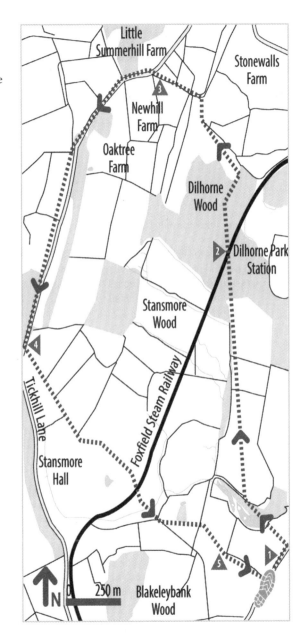

30 Wrinehill and Madeley

START On the Wrinehill to Checkley Road just before the railway bridge, CW3 9BT, GR 753468

DISTANCE 4½ miles (7km)

SUMMARY Easy

MAPS OS Landranger 118

WHERE TO EAT AND DRINK The Crown Inn at Wrinehill (T01270 820472); The Hand and Trumpet at Wrinehill, T01270 820048; The Cuckoo Oak, Madeley, T01952 587324

A well marked route that visits the attractive village of Madeley.

① Walk to Wrinehill, and at the old Blue Bell Inn (now closed) turn right, and head out of the village until the road bears left. Here turn right down a lane to Wrinehill Mill. Go under the railway and follow the lane down past Wrinehill Hall to the farm, and just beyond a crossing of the river.

② Immediately after the crossing, turn left over a small stream and stile to follow the path, which shortly runs diagonally right to a bare hilltop. Follow the remains of a hedgerow over another stile, and keep straight ahead, following the edge of the wood over two further stiles. Go diagonally right. Follow the farm drive to a cattlegrid.

③ After the grid, turn left down the hill past Moss House Farm. Go over the railway bridge, then turn first right and round the estate in Madeley, and left towards the church and the school.

④ Behind the church go left and over the stream. Take the first left turn, and continue towards the village centre past Madeley Old Hall and Pool. Just past The Bridge Inn turn left down Furnace Lane to Lowermill House.

⑤ After 500m, by a left-hand bend, go straight ahead following a footpath sign. Take the right hedge past a hollow, and keep straight on to a field corner. Go over a stile and follow the right hedge; there are fine views across Cheshire. Keep straight ahead to a stile by a pond, then go diagonally left towards the houses. At the road turn left, and walk back into Wrinehill to regain the start point.

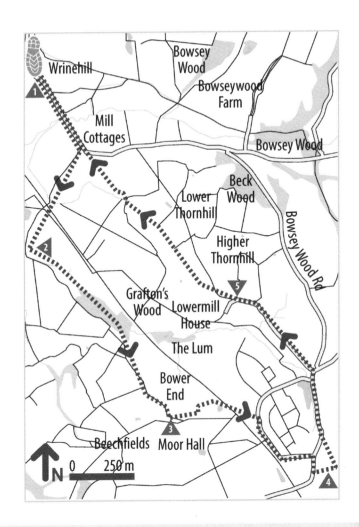

Points of interest

Wrinehill Hall – actually Wrinehill Hall Farm, because it is built on the site of the family hall of the Hawkestone and Egerton families. Madeley Od Hall is a well preserved Jacobean building dated 1647, with an inscription 'You can stay Bed and Breakfast here'.

Ilam, Musden and Blore

START The village of Ilam; park near the monument, DE6 2AZ, GR 135508

MAPS OS Landranger 119

DISTANCE 4½ miles (7km)

WHERE TO EAT AND DRINK National Trust tea rooms, Ilam Hall, 10.30am–5.00pm

SUMMARY Easy with a steep section

1 From the monument, head away from the bridge past ornate cottages on your right, and take the left fork (to Ilam Hall). Immediately afterwards fork left again, and after a few yards turn left through a gate and follow the path first to the church, then through a kissing gate to Ilam Hall. On approaching the hall, turn left and walk down a flight of steps to the river and turn right, following a path known as Paradise Walk. Shortly afterwards you pass the Ilam boil holes and the Battle Stone on the right. Continue through two stiles, and carry on until you get to the River Lodge. Go to the right, on to the road.

2 Here turn left. Follow the road over the bridge at Rushley, and where it bends sharp right, carry straight on through a farmyard. Follow the track uphill towards another farm, and follow it around to the right of this farm.

3 Shortly afterwards the track bends sharp right: take a path on the left that runs steeply uphill. When you reach a slightly sunken, grassed-over track, bear off to the left: this path climbs fairly steeply, bending first to the right, then to the left. Continue ahead until the track peters out, then carry on past a hummock on the left, keeping a wall on the right. Cross a stile by a gate ahead, and then follow the path in a right-hand arc to Upper Musden. Take the path left, out from Upper Musden, and then, bearing left, aim for a green path on the opposite hillside to the left of Hazleton Clump. Head down the slope, cross the remains of two walls and a depression, and then climb on to the green path. Go through two gates and continue to the road where you turn left.

④ Turn left at the crossroads towards Ilam. After passing the parking area, take a path to the right down the hillside; you rejoin the road at the bottom. Turn right and cross the bridge back to the monument.

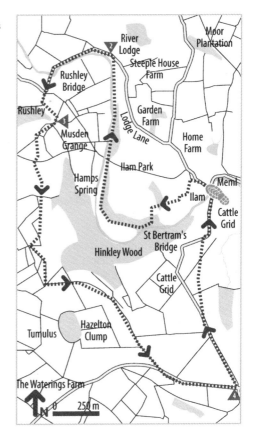

Points of interest

The current Ilam Hall was built in 1840. It is now used as a youth hostel, and there is a National Trust shop and tea rooms.

Ilam boil holes – the waters of the River Manifold go underground further upstream and reappear through the boil holes just before the weir.

The battle stone is thought to be of mid-eleventh-century origin, and associated with the struggle between the Saxons and the Danes.

32 Flash and Gradbach

START In Flash, SK17 0SW, GR 025672

DISTANCE 5 miles (8km)

SUMMARY Easy

MAPS OS Landranger 119 Explorer OL24

WHERE TO EAT AND DRINK The New Inn, at Flash Quarnford, near Buxton (T01298 22941)

An attractive walk over seldom visited territory. There are fine views from the picnic spots.

[1] Leave from the front of the New Inn, and head westwards past the Wesleyan chapel. Continue for about ½ mile downhill to Spring Head Farm, where the farm buildings are on both sides of the road; turn right at a footpath sign, and walk downhill to a stile and footbridge over a small stream. Cross these and follow the track uphill; where it begins to flatten out you will find a small waymark at a junction of footpaths – there is also an obvious stile on the right at this point: go left here, and follow the broad ridge down over stiles and through gates keeping to the left of the gritstone wall, until it is possible to get on to the minor road by Manor Farm.

[2] Turn right here for 50yd, then go left through a stile and follow the stream left to a footbridge and another lane. Turn right along this lane for approximately 500yd; keep left at a fork.

[3] Just past the Gradbach Scout HQ/camp, turn left up a footpath as directed to pass a farmhouse, and continue straight on, following the contour of the hillside to the left; the track is sometimes indistinct. The track eventually becomes a footpath, which leads to Cloughhead; where it joins the road keep going straight ahead, past two road junctions to Gib Torr outcrops and the beginnings of a forested area.

[4] Where the road levels out, turn left for the signposted Ann Roach Farm, and keep to the right side of the escarpment across the moor. Follow the footpath in front of the farm as directed by

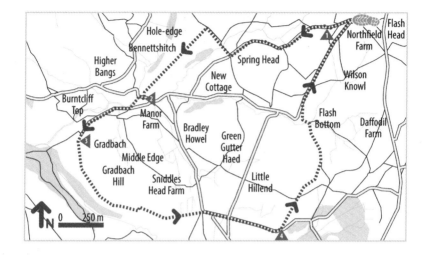

waymarkers, and go through a stile on to a footpath; follow the contour down to Flash Bottom Farm. Follow to the left to pass the farm, then across the farm lane to a stile. Go over and diagonally left across the next field towards a house and a set of steps that leads up to the minor road. Turn right along this road to return to the village of Flash.

Points of interest

At 1,518ft above sea level, Flash is the highest village in England. It gave its name to the slang term for counterfeit money, as in the past 'coiners' had their headquarters here.

33 Wettonmill and Ecton

Start The Hulme End car park, SK17 0EZ, GR 102594

Distance 5 miles (8km)

Summary Fairly easy

Maps OS Landranger 119 Explorer OL24

Where to eat and drink The Manifold Inn at Hulme End, Hartington, www.themanifoldinn.co.uk/default.html (T01298 84537). Also The Tea Junction, www.teajunctionhulmeend.co.uk (T01298 687368)

A circular walk through interesting limestone valley and hills scenery.

① Turn right down the Manifold Way track, and enter an incised gorge. Continue along the track crossing straight over the minor road from Warslow, after which the former Ecton Copper Mine workings appear on the left.

② Cross the footbridge over the Warslow brook, and on meeting the road, carry on straight ahead through a tunnel, but beware of traffic. Then continue along the road approximately 1¼ miles to Wettonmill.

③ At the road junction turn left over the bridge and take the road left to a junction shortly afterwards, where you follow the path straight on, signposted to Back of Ecton. Proceed through a farmyard and carry on up the dry valley ahead, towards Sugarloaf, a limestone outcrop at its head.

④ Walk to the foot of Sugarloaf, then follow the steep path to the left. At the top of the slope, cross the stile ahead and go immediately right over a second stile. Continue on the path, keeping first a fence and then a wall on the right. At the end of the field, carry on with the wall on the left. Go over a stile and on to a junction with a track. Turn left along the track and just before a farmhouse, fork right to go through a wall.

[5] Bear left over a stile and turn right through a gate. Continue up the field ahead, keeping the wall on your right to cross a stile near the top of the incline. From the top, walk straight down the steep slope towards the house ahead, keeping the wall to the left.

[6] At the bottom, turn left on to the road and pass through Back of Ecton to a road junction in the Manifold Valley. Turn right, but at Westside Mill shortly afterwards, turn left on to a footpath footbridge over the river. The path then veers right away from the river and crosses a stile in the fence ahead. Follow the path through the next field heading towards the Manifold Way track. Cross a stile on to the track and turn right back to the car park.

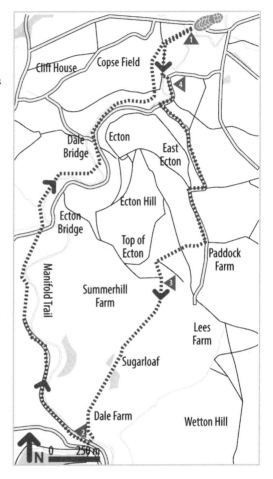

Points of interest

Ecton copper mine was once the deepest mine in Britain, and at 1,400ft one of the deepest in Europe. The mine produced almost 1 million tons of copper, but has not been worked since 1890. Sugarloaf is an unusual, steep and impressive limestone outcrop with good views from its summit across to Ossoms Hill.

34 Roach End and Danebridge

Start Roach End, ST13 8TA, GR 996645

Maps OS Landranger 118 Explorer OL24

Distance 5 miles (8km)

Where to eat and drink Nothing on route

Summary Moderate

A relatively dry walk with some pretty countryside and good views. The last part can feel exposed in windy or cold conditions.

① Go down the lane on your right for a few metres, then over a stile on your left to follow the wall down to the right to the wood edge. Turn left, and take the track that follows the edge for about ⅔ mile until you arrive at the entrance to Lud's Church. Go down through this, and out at the other end. Go left along a path, and then shortly turn right, and walk down to meet a path going left that follows the River Dane but well above it.

② Follow this well marked path through and out of woodlands, passing Back Forest and Back Dane farms, and into woodland again. Continue until you meet the River Dane near Danebridge.

③ Turn left up the road for a hundred yards, then left again at a footpath signed Back Forest and Gradbach. Go up the narrow snicket, bearing left through a small wood, and out over a stile. Head up the field and left of Hangingstone Farm. Bear right along a path above the farm but just below the Hanging Stone, and on past Paddock Farm. Keep to the track as it gradually gains altitude on to the ridge; it eventually arrives at Roach End and the start.

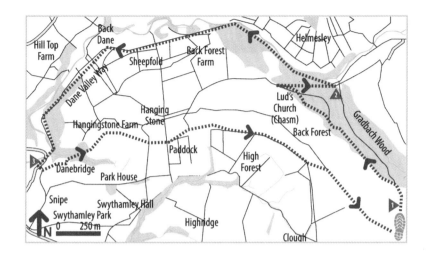

Points of interest

The Hanging Stone is a rock buttress with a dubious history. Lud's Church is a rocky chasm 200ft long and 60ft high. It was used for secret worship by followers of religious reformer John Wycliffe in the 15th century.

START The centre of Brewood, ST19 9DX, GR 883086

DISTANCE 5 miles (8km)

SUMMARY Easy

MAPS OS Landranger 127

WHERE TO EAT AND DRINK There is a selection of pubs and services in Brewood

A fine example of Staffordshire parkland.

[1] Head south along Church Road and bear left at the bottom – a public alleyway can be seen on the right. Take this between houses to an unsurfaced road, where a left turn and an immediate right take you across fields to emerge at Deans Hall Bridge. Turn right across the bridge and follow the unmade road to The Woolley. At the farm continue along the Staffordshire Way, until you come to a stile on the left.

[2] Go over the stile and across the following field to Upper Avenue, the drive leading to Chillington Hall. Cross over the Avenue and, still following the Staffordshire Way signs, cross another field to arrive at a green lane.

[3] Go right, and after passing a white thatched cottage, continue along the track-cum-road to reach a minor surfaced road. Turn right along this road, passing the entrance gate to Chillington Hall, and Horse Paddock Wood, where the road bears left.

[4] At the drive to Chillington Farm, turn right. Pass the farmhouse on your left, and walk between two outbuildings straight ahead into a field. Keep the hedge on your left until it turns 90 degrees left: here you continue straight ahead to a gate on the right-hand side of a stand of trees. Continue to another gate and a cross track. Going right, and pass a house on the left and a small pool on the right. In the field, turn left to follow the garden hedge for about 60yd to its first corner, where a crop-free path leads directly ahead across a field to a gap in the opposite hedge. Through the gap the path bears right and over a wooden bridge. Go up the left-hand side of the next field, arriving at an opening into a

green lane, which brings you to the road at Oakley. Turn right along the road, and then quickly left at the drive to Oakley Farm, to come to a right-hand bend. The route is straight ahead on a clear track until it, too, turns sharp right. Still continuing straight ahead the route is not apparent, so line up on a neatly shaped oak tree in the distance, and walk parallel to Dry Brook Plantation. Continue until you reach a gap in the hedge on to a narrow lane.

5 Turn right and continue along the lane for about ¼ mile until you reach Lee Fields Farm on the right.

6 Shortly after the farm there is a public footpath signposted on the left. Follow this to pass in front of a cottage, and follow the path to arrive at Broom Hall Bridge (Bridge 16) over the canal. Turn right down the towpath, and follow it all the way to Brewood Bridge (Bridge 14); here go up on to the road, and back to Brewood.

Points of interest

Chillington is mentioned in the Domesday Book: it passed in marriage to the Giffard family in the twelfth century, thus beginning an unbroken association of 800 years. The parkland owes much to the work of Capability Brown.

Brewood is a delightful Staffordshire village with a long history, with origins as a Roman fort for the defence of nearby Watling Street.

Circuit of Rudyard Lake

Start The site of the former Rudyard railway station, now the car park for the Rudyard Steam Railway on the B5331 just outside Rudyard, ST13 8PF, GR 955579

Distance 5 miles (8km)

Summary Easy; mostly on good surfaced tracks

Maps OS Landranger 118

Where to eat and drink Refreshments are sometimes available at the Rudyard Lake visitor centre café, www.rudyardlake.com. Open in summer 10am–5pm Mon–Fri and until 6pm at weekends, Oct–Mar weekends only 10am–5pm. The Hotel Rudyard is undergoing change of ownership/refurbishment at the time of the walk

A walk for all seasons, around the Victorian resort of Rudyard.

1 Walk north along the track of the old railway far as the dam on Rudyard Lake. At the dam, cross the footbridge, left, over the dam itself where there are fine views along the lake. Cross the dam, and go up the slope to reach Lake Road.

2 Turn right. In a short while bear left at a signposted public footpath past the back of houses. As you approach the caravan site, go left up the hill. The track narrows: where it levels out, go right to join another path, and descend this for a short way. Just before a house at the bottom of the slope turn left, into woodland. After a few hundred yards the rising track forks: a small path goes off and runs down to reach a tarmaced lane, Reacliffe Road. Turn right and follow this to pass along the back of the lakeside properties and the sailing club. The route continues on to a path, and passes in front of a large house, Cliffe Park. After leaving the grounds of Cliffe Park, continue until you join a surfaced farm track; follow this down to the head of the lake. After crossing the cut that feeds the head of the lake, the lane swings slightly left to a parking area.

3 Here, turn right to join the track of the former railway under a bridge. Follow this for about 2.5 miles to reach the old station and car park.

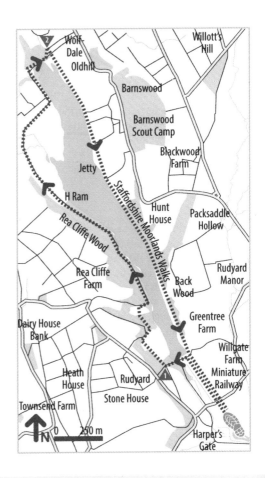

Points of interest

Rudyard Lake was created in 1831 to feed the Trent and Mersey canal system. The lake can sometimes look like the estuary of a small Cornish resort.

Cliffe Park was originally the home of one of the directors of the North Staffordshire Railway company, then it was used as a youth hostel, but now it is a private home again.

Wrottesley Park

START At 856021, the layby on the A41 near the entrance to Wrottesley Golf Club, WV8 2HL

DISTANCE 5 miles (8km)

SUMMARY Easy

MAPS OS Landranger 138 & 139

WHERE TO EAT AND DRINK There is a selection of pubs and services in nearby Codsall

A gentle walk through attractive rolling countryside.

1 Cross the road and walk north along the pavement to a public footpath up steps on the left opposite Shop Lane. Go over the stile and turn left to go around edge of the field. Pass a three-way path sign to a corner straight ahead where a stile takes you into a garden. Pass through the garden left of the pool and emerge on to a wide track. Go straight ahead as far as a Y-Junction.

2 Take the right-hand fork towards a shed, and turn right to follow the edge of Simmonds Wood. Where the track goes right, walk straight ahead through a hunter's gate, then on and through another gate into a green lane; this passes the Coach House and arrives at a track junction by Kingswood Bank Farm. Turn left in front of the semi-detached houses, and continue along the farm track to Wrottesley Lodge Farm. Go through the farm and head for the edge of Birch Coppice, and from there towards another stand of trees.

3 Before reaching the trees turn left, by an electricity pole, keeping a hedge on your left. Follow the track for a mile to Bradshaws Farm. Pass to the left of the houses ahead to reach a tarmac track. Turn right, and then left along the edge of some trees. Soon the track swings right to emerge from the trees with a large pool on the right, and Wrottesley Hall on the left. Follow the track past the Hall, and continue to a left bend, which you follow to join the Staffordshire Way. Soon climb a stile on the left, and turn right along the drive to reach the golf course. To the left is the Club House

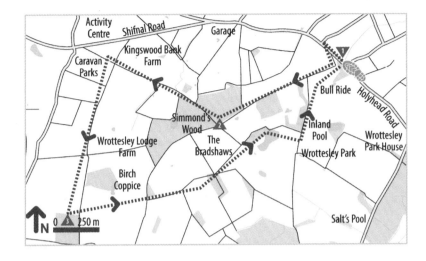

and a Staffordshire Way sign. Follow it through woodland, over a sleeper bridge and on to the path you walked earlier, right round the field to the road. Turn right and retrace your steps to the layby.

Points of interest

Wrottesley Hall: formerly the home of the Wrottesley family, the manor pre-dates the Norman Conquest. The old Hall was destroyed by fire towards the end of the last century, along with some priceless literary treasures.

Okeover, Blore and Coldwall Bridge

START On the roadside to Okeover Bridge near Mapleton, or in the village, DE6 2AB, GR 165482

DISTANCE 5 miles (8km)

SUMMARY Moderate

MAPS OS Landranger 119

WHERE TO EAT AND DRINK The Okeover Arms, Mapleton, http://theokeover. co.uk (T01335 350305); food is served Mon–Fri 12.00–3.00pm and 6.00–9.00pm, Sat and Sun 12.00–9.00pm

A steady ascent through Okeover Park to the hamlet of Blore, with fine views towards Dovedale.

1 Cross the bridge: on the left is a ladder stile. Cross this and veer left: the route crosses a road, then follow a footpath just to the left of a group of trees. Follow this uphill and through a timber gate towards a derelict house. Go straight ahead to a gap in the wood, cross the stile, go along the wood edge, and aim slightly right across a field to a gate with a footpath signpost. Go through this into the next field; swerve round an enclosure in the middle of the field, and continue to a stile on to a track leading to a farm.

2 Go through the gate at the end of the track and turn right. Go through another gate on the right of a farm, then cross another stile to reach a path along the left field boundary. Follow the path across three fields to join a walled track to Woodhouses Farm. Go through the gate, pass the farm buildings, and you will reach a narrow lane that leads to Blore. Continue to a crossroads.

3 Here turn right and follow the road, which is an old eighteenth-century turnpike road, to Coldwall Farm. Turn left down the farm drive to a rough track beyond, and go into a field through a gate. A footpath descends steeply in a direct line to Coldwall Bridge.

4 Turn right through a stile in the right wall on the approach to the bridge; follow this path to a track along the right bank of the

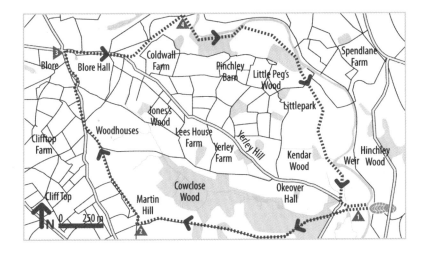

river. Follow this through a small wood and along a clear path that swings away from the river and into another small wood. As you enter the wood, take a footpath waymarked to the right and up to a stile. Go over this and continue in a similar direction to reach a track adjacent to a farm. Turn right along the track for 100yd, then go left to cross a stile. Head across the large field to a stile in the left corner just down from a copse. Cross the next field in the same direction; you will get to the river again on your left, and from here, the path goes straight across the field to an old mill building and the road. Turn left along the road, then left off the road and across the bridge to regain the start.

Points of interest

Blore has a small fourteenth-century church, and a sixteenth-century hall.

Rushton Spencer and Gun End

Start Staffordshire County Council car park in the old railway yard at Rushton Spencer, SK11 0QU, GR 936624

Distance 5½ miles (8.5km)

Summary Moderate/Easy

Maps OS Landranger 119

Where to eat and drink The Knot Inn, Rushton Spencer, (T01260 226238)

A varied walk following an old railway track and canal cut, and over remote hillside pastures.

① Leave the car park past the renovated station building and cross the road to follow the Staffordshire waymarkings north along the old railway track for ¾ mile to a path down the embankment left, signposted the Staffordshire way, by a bridge. Turn right to follow the Gritstone Trail under the bridge. Cross the road and head across fields; the path takes a sharp right up to a stile where you meet the canal cut. Go left to stroll along the cut for about 1¼ miles to a weir and footbridge.

② Turn away from the footbridge and take the stepped path over a wooden stile to the left of the gate in front of Gig Hall. Once up the steep bank, head over a wooden stile and fields to Hollinhall Farm. Go to the right of a farm barn and then left, and follow signposts round to the right of the farm and through a paddock; join the lane and go right towards Gun End main road. Before the junction is reached, turn right to go alongside a bungalow, where the lane peters out.

③ Cross a concrete footbridge and go through a gate to a green lane. Shortly on the left you will find a wooden stile: take the path beyond this to Toft Hall. Go over a stile and into the court of Toft Hall; turn right and leave the court over another stile, and continue across more fields and stiles to join a lane at Heaton.

④ Turn right and right again, and take a stile shortly on the left. Follow the boundary to the bottom left of the field and go through

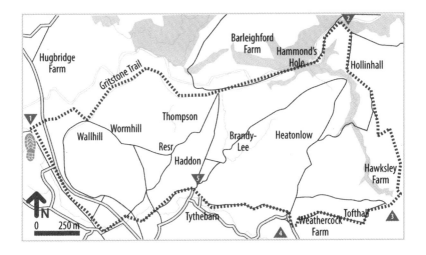

a squeezer and other stiles; the route may be directed by electrified fencing across the farm track to a signposted stile. Go over the stile and pass between telegraph poles to head across and down to a squeezer. Beyond this go around to the left of a farm and join the farm lane; follow this left to the second junction, by another farm.

⑤ Cross the road and turn left behind a hedge and go over stiles. Continue diagonally right, staying to the right of a stream and high up on the bank; cross more stiles and descend to a footbridge. Cross this to reach a farm and pass the farmhouse through a gate. Go down the lane left at the junction with another lane to cross the main road and finish back at the car park.

40

Haughton and Berry Ring

START The car park by the bridge in Station Road, Haughton, ST18 9HE, GR 862214

DISTANCE 5 miles (8km)

SUMMARY A fairly easy walk

MAPS OS Landranger 127

WHERE TO EAT AND DRINK A selection of pubs in Haughton, in particular The Bell, T01785 780301, www.thebellhaughton.co.uk; and The Shropshire Inn, T01785 780904, www.theshropshireinnhaughton.co.uk/

A fine walk over pleasant agricultural land.

① From the car park go right, under the bridge, and follow the old Wellington/Stafford railway bed for 1½ miles to a minor lane with a cottage in front and what used to be a level crossing.

② Here go right, and immediately right again, and follow the track to the left around the right-hand side of Stallbrook Hall Farm (do not follow the farm track back parallel with the railway bed), and through a pedestrian gate. Arriving at a field edge you will see, to your left, a solitary tree that has been waymarked with yellow paint. Make your way to this, and then head across the field to a hunter's gate in the opposite hedge; in the next field keep to the left of another waymarked oak tree. In the field after this, continue straight ahead to the corner of a derelict farm; pass to the right of the barn and through another hunter's gate, and then past two oak trees to another hunter's gate. Ahead is Berry Ring, and to your left, Stafford Castle. Following the line of the yellow arrow, cross the next field to a metal gate in the hedge.

③ Here you join the farm road that takes you up to the tarmac lane around Berry Ring. Shortly you reach the drive to Dearnsdale Farm. Follow this down to a gate just to the left of the farmhouse.

④ Here the official public footpath goes right and between two barns, and then left along the hedged and fenced track. However, a diversion is under consideration/negotiation, and instead you may be directed

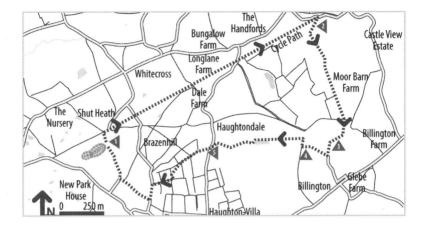

to follow diversion signs that take you round the left-hand side of the farmhouse to join the same hedged and fenced track. Follow this, passing a pool on the left, and go through the gate at the end of the track; turn left and walk for a few yards to a double gate. Go through this, and cross over a stream; then go right to follow the opposite bank to the field corner. Here go left for a few yards to where, on the right, there is a fence stile. Go over this, passing between the house and the garage, and cross the drive to a gate into a field. In the field go left and follow the hedge until you emerge at a lane.

⑤ Turn left and walk for 20yd, when you will see a fence stile on the right. Cross the stile and head across the field towards a gate and a wooden stile. Go over this, and follow the direction of the yellow arrow along the line of the hedge; in the next field walk diagonally left to a corner stile and on to a service track. Follow the track to a lane, and turn left to a public footpath sign on the right, immediately before the 30mph sign. Go right over the fence stile and along the footpath, following the edge of the housing estate, to Station Road. Turn right along the road to reach the car park.

Points of interest

Berry Ring is an ancient defensive hill fort on a natural hillock.

41

Milldale, Stanshope and Alstonefield

Start The public car park at Milldale, DE6 2AY, GR 136548

Distance 5 miles (8km)

Summary Moderate

Maps OS Landranger 119, or Explorer OL24

Where to eat and drink The George, Alstonefield, www.thegeorgeatalstonefield.com, (T01335 310 205), Mon–Thurs 11.30am–3pm and 6pm–11pm, Fri and Sat 11.30am–11pm, Sun 12pm–9.30pm; check website or by phone for food times

A walk with beautiful views of Dove Dale from the less used Staffordshire bank.

[1] Walk down from the car park into Milldale, where there is a delightful packhorse bridge and information barn. Between the gents toilet and Mill Cottage is a narrow path that rises steeply for approximately 30yd before turning left along the hillside. The path is clear and well stiled, in the early stages giving fine views down into Dove Dale before descending to continue along the river's edge. Follow the riverside path; shortly after passing Dove Holes, over on the far bank, you reach a wall with a slit stile.

[2] Ignore the stile and turn right along a clear path up Hall Dale. At the top, cross the stile into a field where the path veers right to cross two more stiles before reaching a rough track by a footpath sign. Turn left; you will soon reach a road.

[3] At the road, turn right: this is the track between Stanshope Hall and the farm. Proceed along this, and descend to the road in Hope Dale. Cross to a stile opposite, and continue steeply up the hillside; swing left at the top, and follow the boundary wall to a stile and gate. Go over the stile and keep straight ahead, turning right at the road and immediately right again to reach Alstonefield village green.

[4] Continue past the green, turning right at the end to pass the Manor House and church, beyond which the road narrows to the

packhorse way known as Millway Lane. The lane descends to the riverside in Milldale where the walk started.

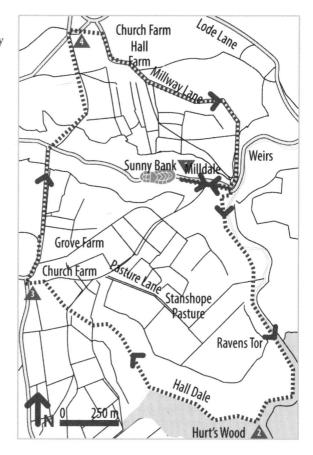

Points of interest

In Milldale the packhorse bridge, known as Viator's Bridge, is referred to in the 1676 edition of Izaak Walton's *Compleat Angler*.

Alstonefield was originally a Saxon settlement. It was once a busy market town – its charter was granted in 1308 – and the crossroads of several packhorse ways. The church is the third on the same site and has a Norman south doorway and chancel arch, and fine seventeenth-century pews.

Six Lane Ends and Turner's Pool

START Six Lane Ends, DE6 5HB, GR 963618

MAPS OS Landranger 118

WHERE TO EAT AND DRINK Nothing on route

DISTANCE 5 miles (8km)

SUMMARY Easy/Moderate

A reasonable all-year-round walk with unusual views of the Roaches estate.

1 Go east along the lane with a farm on the left, and head for the crest of the ridge. From here on there are good views of the Roaches estate. Continue down the lane.

2 When you get to a wood, turn left following the lane towards Oldhay Top farm. At the left bend just before the farm, head straight down over a field to a step stile in the wall. Cross this and follow the direction indicated down into a hollow.

3 Here there is a small stream on the right: go over the slab to cross it, then over a wooden stile beyond. Turn left and follow the signed footpath to Wetwood and Meerbrook, passing through farm gates near a cowshed to join the farm lane, turning left to meet a road.

4 Turn left and follow the public footpath along the private farm lane for just over 1 mile to reach Meadows Farm.

5 At Meadows Farm turn left over two stiles to a paddock, then turn left along the farm lane and continue into a field; keep to the right of the fence to cross a stile and small stream. Head across the next field to cross another stream by a right-angled fence. Then go diagonally left, up the bank, then down and up a dip to a stile by the edge of a wood. Follow the wood edge over two more stiles to reach the north side of Turner's Pool.

6 Go past the pool, and after 100yd take a stile on the left (just before a barn on the left), and follow a path over a paddock to a small stream with

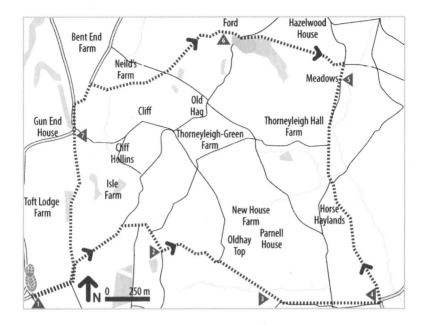

a footbridge and stile beyond. Once over these, head diagonally right up to a gate; go through this, and turn left along the field boundary. Go through another gate, and make for a stile ahead. Go over this, and on to another gate by some holly trees. Continue until you pick up a lane, and pass Nield's Farm on its left to reach the farm lane. Follow this to a road: go left and continue for approximately 300yd until you reach a sharp right-hand bend.

⑦ Take the lane straight ahead, with Gun End cottage on your left. Continue along the green lane past a wood to meet the roadway, where you turn right to regain the start.

Points of interest

The Roaches estate – all the splendid ridge and surrounding moorland is in the hands of the Peak District National Park.

43 Calf Heath and Shareshill

START Long Moll's canal bridge,
WV10 7DL, GR929088

DISTANCE 5 miles (8km)

SUMMARY Easy

MAPS OS Landranger 127

WHERE TO EAT AND DRINK The Dog and
Partridge, Calf Heath T01902 276756
www.dogandpartridgecalfheath.
com

A fine walk past people messing about in boats.

1 From Long Moll's bridge, follow the road west to arrive at
Deepmore Mill Farm. The road ahead is now a green lane, which you
follow to a junction: here go left to arrive at Moat House bridge and
canal. Cross the bridge, and shortly take the right fork to a tarmac
lane.

2 Go right along the lane for 25yd to a stile on the left with a
footpath sign. Follow the path to meet another one and go right,
through the graveyard, to the church and explore the village.
For the return journey, retrace your steps through the graveyard,
except instead of going left along the route of the inward journey, go
straight ahead to a stile and across a field to a narrow lane.

3 Turn left, and continue for ½ mile to a junction. Go straight
ahead along an unmade lane, passing Lower Latherford Farm on the
right, to arrive back at Moat House bridge. Take the towpath right
along the canal, and so back to Long Moll's bridge and the start.

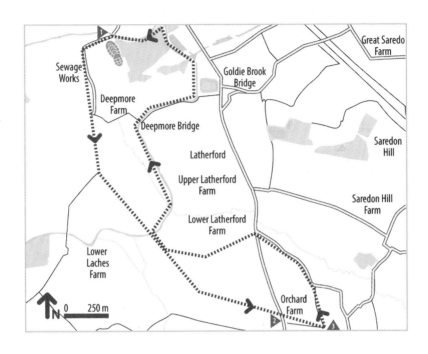

Betley and Heighley

Start Near the Swan in Betley, CW3 9AB, GR 754485

Distance 5 miles (8km)

Summary Easy

Maps OS Landranger 118

Where to eat and drink The Swan, Betley, www.theswanbetley.co.uk, and T01270 820322 for opening times

A well marked and delightful walk.

[1] Descend Common Lane, and after 150m go over a stream and left over a stile. Cross the field and another stile. Betley Mere is on your left. Continue down to steps over a marshy area. At the second footbridge, go diagonally left for the corner of a wood, and across to the right edge of the wood ahead. Go over a stile, through trees and over a footbridge to an open area. Continue in a line with the stream, crossing two footbridges.

[2] Go right over another footbridge, and immediately left over a stile. Follow the line of two ditches, go over a stile on the right and then left join Cracow Moss by a black-and-white house. Go up the hill to the main road. Turn right through Wrinehill and at the end of the village go left at a footpath sign.

[3] Cross the field to the end of the hedge on the left. Go over a stile and turn right over two stiles and a footbridge. Continue left along the hedge, then right along the field boundary to a stile, which you cross.

[4] Turn immediately right to another stile. Go left past a ruin, and after 20m, right over a stile across a field, then over a stile by a gate. Head towards a cottage and lane. Go along this, then sharp right and left to a forest track in Bowsey Wood.

[5] Turn right through a small gate just before the farm, go over a footbridge and up through a wood to a road. Go left for 50m, and left again down a minor road. Follow this for 1km to the cottages at Adderley Green.

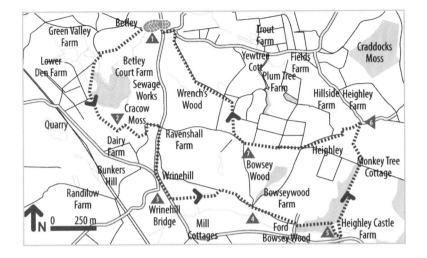

[6] Go left over a stile, up the hill, over another stile and follow the hedge. Go left, and immediately right over more stiles to make for a small woodland. Go through, and head diagonally left to the far corner of the field. Take the right-hand of two stiles, and follow the hedge over two more stiles. Continue up the slope.

[7] Halfway down the next slope go right over a stile, then diagonally left to another. Do not cross the stile, but continue right along the hedge to a stile in the corner. Go diagonally left to the left field corner. Go over a stile on the left and cross a narrow field to steps down, a footbridge, and steps up. Continue directly across the field to the far right. Go over a stile and follow the hedge into the village of Betley past the cricket ground and church. At the top, turn left past the church to a new road.

Points of interest

 Betley Mere is a Site of Special Scientific Interest under the care of the Nature Conservancy Council.

Betley: almost the whole village has been designated a conservation area. The church is thirteenth century, and is one of the best examples in the county of a timber-framed church.

START The layby on the road between Ramshorn and the B5417, opposite Green Lane, ST10 3BT, GR 080457

DISTANCE 5 miles (8km)

SUMMARY Fairly easy

MAPS OS Landranger 119, Explorer 259

WHERE TO EAT AND DRINK There are various choices at Alton or Oakamoor

A walk mainly through fields, woodland and common land.

1 Cross the road and go down Green Lane to Ramshorn Road. Turn left to the hamlet of Ramshorn, where the route turns down to the right past Gander Well. From here the view is extensive. Go down past the well.

2 Go through metal gates adjacent to a cattle grid. Follow the field boundary and woods on the left to a wooden stile, and cross this to enter the woods. Carry on down to join a lane up to and through Cote Farm yard. Shortly after leaving the farm yard, go left down a track and cross a small stream. Go over a stile on the right, and up through a plantation and on to Wootton Lane. Turn right to Farley, and at the telephone kiosk turn right into Hay Bank Lane. Keep left at the fork, and cross another farm track.

3 Where the lane swings slightly right by a barn to a house there is a gate on the left. Do not cross the stile, but go through the gate on to Longshaw Lane. This can be poorly defined, but roughly it follows a brook, goes over a footbridge, and up to a tall deer-proof gate. Go through this gate and veer right towards an oak tree to meet a farm lane. Follow this to the left; go through more deer-proof gates to reach Ramshorn Road. Cross over the road on to a track into the woodland on Ramshorn Common. The path is not well defined and needs care, but roughly you follow the line of old concrete fence posts.

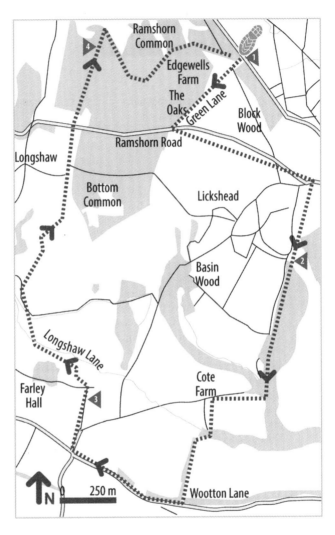

④ Where these finish, curve round to the right. Keeping sight of the dense woodland over to your right, find a track clearing through the trees and occasional waymarkers; the route becomes easier to follow as you approach Edgewells Farm. Follow the track to the left of the farm up and out on to a road. Turn right to the layby at the starting point.

START The car park at the southern end of Madeley near the church, CW3 9PQ, GR 773443

DISTANCE 5 miles (8km)

SUMMARY Easy

MAPS OS Landranger 118

WHERE TO EAT AND DRINK The Cuckoo Oak T 01952 587324; The Six Bells T01952 271696

An enjoyable walk with surprisingly good views, and passing places of industrial and historic interest.

① Go left out of the car park, and left along the main road over the railway bridge. Follow the road for a short way and take the track on the left marked as a bridle path. After 200m, continue on an unmade lane, passing to the left of two ponds. Go through an iron gate, and cross to another iron gate; go through a cutting into an open field. Pass through a gateway to the left of a large iron gate, and keeping the hedge on the right, go to another large iron gate and along a lane between hedges. Go straight on past New Terrace Farm on your right, and keep to the right of the small cottage into the field. Continue with a small stream to your right, then veer left towards a footbridge over the river. Go under the bridge of the disused railway and through a gate. Turn right after the bridge, and follow the embankment of the old wagon route to a lane. Take this lane to the village of Aston.

② Keep turning left in the village till the road makes a right turn: in front of you there is a lane that goes straight on, heading to Lunts Farm. Bear left at this point at a footpath sign. Go between hedges for 50m, then right and eventually cross a stile.

③ Keep the hedge on the left, and cross two more stiles and an open field. Go diagonally right and aim for a stile to the right of a large oak tree, and go straight across the next field to another stile. Cross the footbridge and stile and go straight ahead, keeping to the right of a pool. Go diagonally left here to another footbridge and stile. Go over these and turn left. Go over another stile into the disused railway cutting. Turn right

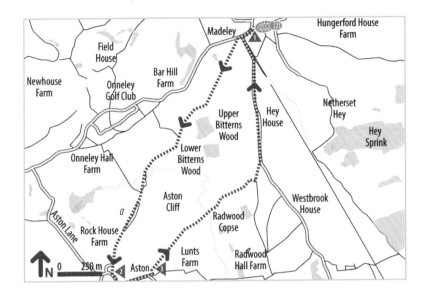

for about 25m and go up the opposite bank and over a stile. Take a line to the right to a point some 100m along the field boundary from the railway bank. Go over a stile and footbridge, and make for the site of the moat and gardens of the ruined Madeley Manor. Go over the second bridge and up the track for 50m. Now go diagonally right to the field corner and over a stile on to a road. Go left along the road for about 1.5km until you reach a footbridge over the railway. Go over this bridge into a field by a gate. Cross the small footbridge and turn diagonally left across the field to another gate to go down the track and left to Madeley car park.

Points of interest

Madeley Manor was originally built in the fourteenth century; it was rebuilt in Tudor/Jacobean style, but sadly is now a ruin.

Madeley is a well maintained village with several fine buildings, one of which is the school on the opposite side of the road to All Saints Church. It was founded to provide free education to the boys and girls of the parishes of Madeley and Mucklestone.

Upper Longdon and Flaxley Green

START At the forest edge in Upper
Longdon, WS15 1PZ, GR 058145

DISTANCE 5½ miles (8.8km)

SUMMARY Easy

MAPS OS Landranger 128

WHERE TO EAT AND DRINK The
Chetwynd Arms in Upper
Longdon, www.facebook.com/
thechetwyndarms, (T01543 490266)

Most of this walk is within the Cannock Chase AONB; it also touches
the urban fringe of Rugeley.

1 Walk towards the village, and almost opposite Shavers Lane is an
unsurfaced lane going downhill. Follow this: it soon becomes a green
lane and meets a T-junction of tracks. Turn left, then shortly on the
right cross a stile to follow a footpath across fields heading for trees just
visible over the rise. Go over the stile and follow the path along the edge
of the treeline, and cross another stile into a field. Keep going straight
ahead downhill, then bear slightly left to a footbridge across a stream.
Cross this and the stile beyond. Go a few paces left and cross a stile on
to a narrow fenced path rising up to an old railway bed, which is now a
footpath. Go straight across and follow the footpath around and uphill
with the hedge on your left, until you get to a road. Turn right and go
100yd, then take the signposted footpath on the left between houses and
industrial premises. Soon you will reach a junction of paths: bear right,
and follow the path around. Where a track/path joins from the right,
continue ahead to Coppice Lane.

2 Here turn left. Follow this along, bearing left at a fork to reach a road
at a cemetery. Turn left to the car park at Flaxley Green.

3 Go through the parking area to the right, and take a track up left
to the ridge top and a junction of tracks. Go left along a track until it
narrows at a clump of gorse bushes, beyond which turn right and drop
steeply down a waymarked path to another track. Turn right to reach a
road. Turn right here, and shortly on the left take a signposted path into
trees. Beyond these go left on a track which initially swings right into
more trees, and further into the forest and up to meet Startley Lane.

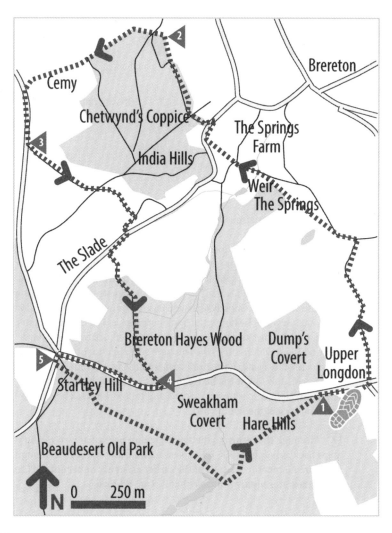

④ Turn right and continue to the crossroads, where you turn left.

⑤ Almost immediately turn left on to a forest track, and follow this for approximately ¾ mile to Horsepasture Pool. Turn left and stay with this main track as it swings left and then right. Continue back along the metalled road and to Upper Longdon.

The Carry Lane Track

START On the north side of the A518, about 3 miles south-west of Uttoxeter, GR 052313

DISTANCE 5 miles (8km)

SUMMARY Easy

MAPS OS Landranger 128

WHERE TO EAT AND DRINK Nothing on route

An easy walk away from roads.

[1] The route is well defined for almost the whole of its length and can easily be seen from where you park the car. Follow the wide track, which can be rutted by farm vehicles and muddy at times. After a while you meet a better surfaced track; the route continues straight ahead along this into woodland. Shortly after you pass a house – the only one along the route. Beyond the house the track becomes less well defined, but is still easy to follow: keep to the hedge on your left. After about ¼ mile the woodland widens off to the left: here veer right to follow a small watercourse to a gate in the right corner of the woodlands. Go through into a field, and follow the hedge on the left. Where the edge turns left, go straight across towards a tree, and follow the track beyond to eventually meet the B5027 road.

[2] Although the return to the starting point necessitates retracing your steps back along the track, it is a pleasant and easy walk. Even though there are no recorded details of the earlier existence or uses of the Carry Lane track, it is highly probable that it is an old road.

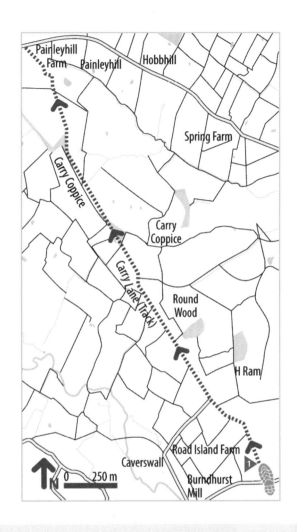

Points of interest

The track runs approximately parallel with the small River Blythe, which is half a mile or so away to the left. Between the track and the river and close to Caverswall there is a moated site, but no written records of its history exist as far as is known.

Start The picnic site at the old Froghall Wharf, ST10 2HJ, GR 026476

Distance 5 miles (8km)

Summary Easy

Maps OS Landranger 119

Where to eat and drink Fox and Goose, at Foxt (T01538 266415); phone for opening times

A pleasant walk with a sense of exploration on the outward journey and the knowledge that there is an easy level route back.

①　Go over the canal bridge and then left and down on to the Caldon Canal bank. After the cottages on the right drop down again to a footbridge; go over this and up the other side. Turn right along a track into Moseymoor Wood, following Blackbank Brook. The path steepens and passes a lake on the right, then continues uphill to a farm gate. Go through into a field, and follow the hedge on the right to a road. Turn right and continue for a few hundred yards.

②　Turn off left at a stile to a farm track that runs left and uphill. Ignore a later track going off right, and continue straight on to a stile in a wall. Cross into a second field and follow the tracks across the middle to a gap in a wall. Go through into a third field and across to a gate, then into a fourth field and diagonally right to a wall, and cross this into a fifth field.

③　Turn right along the wall to a gate into a sixth field; follow the wall on the right. When it turns right, go straight on into the woods, and take a wide track going down to a stream. Cross a stile and footbridge, and go up steps to a stile. Cross into a field and go uphill to the top corner near Booth's Wood Farm, and out over a fence. Cross a farm track to a stile. Cross into a field and go diagonally left to another track. Go to a stile in the stone wall on the left; cross into a farmyard and go diagonally left to a gate and another farm track. Turn left off the track over wire into a field, and follow the hedge on the left to a gate in the top left corner. Go into

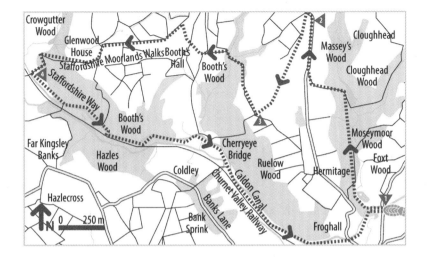

another field, and follow the hedge on the right to its end. Turn left, and go out through hedge gaps to a farm track. Turn right and go through a gate into Glenwood House farmyard. Turn off left at the barn, and go through a gate into a field. Keep to the hedge on the right, but when it curves right, go diagonally left across the field to a stile in the middle of the fence. Cross the stile into woods – ignore the path to the right – and follow the path slightly left; you will meet a new path where you turn right. This path goes downhill to steps and on to the Caldon Canal.

(4) Turn left along the canal and follow it back to Froghall.

Cheddleton Station and Consall Forge

START At the road junction adjacent to Cheddleton Station, ST10 2HA, GR 982520

DISTANCE 5 miles (8km)

SUMMARY Easy

MAPS OS Landranger 118

WHERE TO EAT AND DRINK The Boat Inn in Basford Bridge Lane, Cheddleton, To1538 360683; Mon–Thurs and Sun 12am–11pm, Fri and Sat 12am–12pm

A delightful walk through our early industrial past.

⬜1 Cross the level crossing and bridge to reach The Boat Inn; pass in front of the pub on a footpath to Wetley Rocks. The route gradually rises away from the canal up to Felt House Farm, crossing a stream on the way up through a narrow wood. Pass in front of the farm buildings, and take the lane heading slightly uphill and westwards. At the lane end continue in a similar line down to and over the stream, and up across several fields to reach a road. Turn left here, and follow the road to a T-junction.

⬜2 Turn left and follow the road through the hamlet of Consall, and then left towards Consall Forge. After about half a mile the road bends sharp right: just before the entrance to the Nature Park, take a footpath on the left. Go across fields and through former spoil heaps, then right across another field to reach the steps down to the old furnaces and The Black Lion pub.

⬜3 Go immediately left along the canalized part of the River Churnet, past the old furnaces. At the lock where the River Churnet and the canal separate, go over the lock bridge and continue along the towpath on the east side of the Cauldon Canal. You soon reach The Boat Inn, where you turn right to regain the starting point. You might like to visit the Churney Valley Railway.

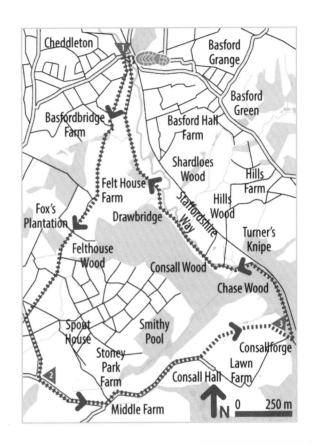

Points of interest

🔍 The old furnaces are the remains of old lime-burning kilns, now largely cleared of vegetation.

The Cauldon Canal is a 17-mile-long canal which was restored and now has a second life as a pleasure boat canal. There is plenty of wildlife along its banks.

The Churney Valley Railway is run by a railway preservation society with some steam trains.

The 'Ha-Ha' Walk

START Millford Common, ST17 0UH, GR 972211

DISTANCE 5 miles (8km)

SUMMARY Easy

MAPS OS Landranger 127

WHERE TO EAT AND DRINK Barley Mow in Milford, T01785 665230, daily 11am–11pm

A small hill at the start is followed by an easy flat walk.

① Go away from the car park across the grass to the A513 and the entrance to Shugborough House. Walk along the road to the speed de-restriction sign and take the path on the left, by a stone wall, going uphill. At the top, pass a covered water tank on the left, and take the track going downhill towards the road. Walk along the road and turn left on to a tarmac track passing White Barn Farm.

② Follow the track as it turns left and enters Shugborough Park. After crossing the railway you can turn right and go on to the 'Ha-Ha' walk, which is a path that takes a half circle around a walled garden, coming back to the main path again. Resume the walk along the main track past the working farm to reach a junction in front of the house. At certain times of the year you can veer left towards the house, and there are paths around the back leading to pleasant gardens by the River Sow. However, if this area is closed you continue along the track, with views of the front of the house to the left, and proceed ahead to cross an old stone bridge.

③ After the bridge turn down on the right to the canal bank, and go left under the bridge and along the towpath. After about 500yd you arrive at a humpback bridge crossing the Staffordshire canal, which here joins the Trent Mersey Canal. Go to the right and under the bridge, and left along the towpath of the Staffordshire canal. Keep on this towpath for 1½ miles, passing where it crosses above the River Trent by an aqueduct and where it broadens out, becoming like a lake (to pacify local objections when it was being built). Eventually you come to a bridge carrying a road; on the opposite side of the canal is a modern house in extensive gardens.

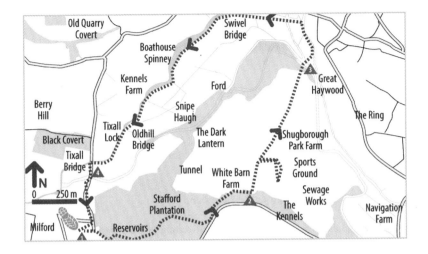

4 Just beyond the bridge take the steps up to the Tixall road. Go right along the road, crossing over the railway line, and continue to Millford where the walk started.

Points of interest

Shugborough House – charges apply if you wish to see the house, its museum and farm.

You won't see anything funny in the 'Ha-Ha' walk, as some people expect: 'ha-ha' is the name for a sunken path.

START **The obelisk in Tixall, ST18 0XS, GR 976226**

DISTANCE **5½ miles (8.8km)**

SUMMARY **Easy**

MAPS **OS Landranger 127**

WHERE TO EAT AND DRINK **The Clifford Arms, T 01889 881321, http://cliffordarms.co.uk**

A relaxing walk through varied countryside.

[1] Leave the obelisk and walk south along the lane signed for Millford. In ⅓ mile, take the lane on the left signed Tixall Lock Farm, and walk along this to the canal bridge. Go right, and follow the canal towpath for the next 2½ miles to St Thomas Bridge (Bridge 101).

[2] Here you leave the canal and go right along the road. Pass over two further bridges and continue uphill to reach a road junction by a crematorium. Here turn right, and almost immediately left along a No Through Road signed for Hanyards. Follow this peaceful little lane for just over a mile until just before the left turn for Upper Hanyards Farm.

[3] Almost at the top of the rise, and before the left bend in the farm lane, is a gate on the right giving a view to Tixall Park Pool and the expanse of Cannock Chase. Go through the gate and head for the distant electricity pylon in line with the far left corner of the pool. On your way you pass two gates, followed by a third into a big field leading to the pool. Turn left on a bearing of 150 degrees, slightly right of the Tixall Gatehouse: this line will bring you to the right-hand edge of a very small and narrow reservoir. Go forward to a gate and lane, which is now very evident. Turn right into Tixall, and spend some time exploring this enigmatic place before turning right along the road back to the obelisk.

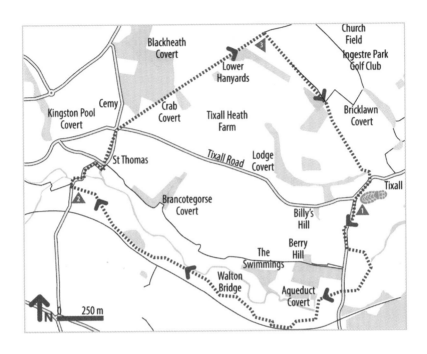

Ordley Brook and Stanton

START The layby on the A52, GR 145470

DISTANCE 6 miles (9.5km)

SUMMARY Moderate

MAPS OS Landranger 127

WHERE TO EAT AND DRINK The Dog & Partridge, Swinscoe (1 mile up the A52 road), www.dogandpartridge. co.uk, T01335 343183

An interesting, little known walk.

1️⃣ Walk up the road on the same side as the layby, and just beyond a small farm take a signposted footpath on the left. Go through the paddock, and halfway into the field beyond, turn right along another footpath to reach a stile. Go through three more fields in a similar direction and into a fourth field until you almost reach the road – but then turn left across the same field heading towards a farm. Go through a gate towards the farm following a track, first to the right and then left behind the farm.

2️⃣ Follow this track to Ellishill Farm. Go left through the farm and follow a boundary on the left.

3️⃣ After a new track coming up from the right, leave the left boundary and start to drop down the contours to the right to a stile next to a gate. Cross this and go left through woods until eventually you reach a stile. Go across, and walk the length of the field, keeping right to reach a stile on to the road. Cross the stile and go right, uphill.

4️⃣ Just past a left-hand bend take a signposted path on the left, and shortly go through a gate into woods. After about ⅓ mile you come to a crossroads of footpaths where there is a small post with waymarkers.

5️⃣ Go right, and up a steep bank to a stile. Go over this and turn right, and across a big field to another stile. Cross it, and head in a similar direction uphill to a gate with a waymarker. Go through, and keeping to the wall on the right, walk until you get to another gate; go through this, and continue diagonally through the next and across the following field until you reach a wooden stile near a stream. Cross this, and follow the field boundary on the right uphill and through the next two fields, and on to Honeywell Lane.

6 Turn right, and walk to a T-junction where you turn left; continue for approximately 150yd: you will reach Flather Lane on the right. Go along this lane until it ends at a farm gate. Go through into a field, and follow the hedge on the left for a short while until you can follow the well defined path downhill to a stile and stepping stones. Cross here, and follow the path over a second footbridge and up stone steps. Cross a

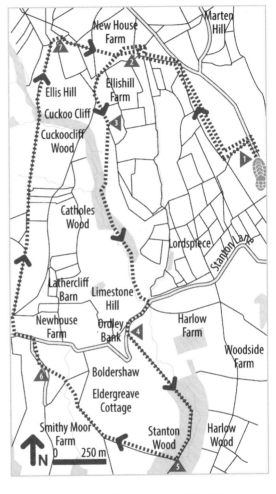

stile at the top into a very big field; here there is the impressive Ellis Hill. Go diagonally left up and across the hill following a line of electricity poles to a metal gated stile almost in the top left corner.

7 Go through, and turn right to a wooden stile in the right boundary. Go over this and veer left to another stile, and proceed in a similar direction across fields to Ellishill Farm; from here you can retrace your steps back to the start.

Gnosall and Shelmore Wood

START In Gnosall, ST20 0ET, GR 828215

DISTANCE 6 miles (9.5km)

SUMMARY Easy

MAPS OS Landranger 127

WHERE TO EAT AND DRINK The Royal Oak in Newport Road, Gnosall, T01785 822362

A very easy walk through varied landscape.

1 Leave Gnosall along Knightly Road, and take the second turn left along the No Through Road. At a fork in the lane go left, and at the next junction go left again, down past Timbersbrook Cottage, and follow the unfenced road across the common. When you come to a pool on the right, the road ahead becomes a track, then narrows to a clear footpath.

2 Continue on this, and cross a footbridge and a stile to arrive at a second stile near Nut Wood. Cross this and turn right with the fence for a few yards to a third stile. Cross it to pick up your original line. Now go left, with the hedge on your left, to the field corner, turning left and right through gates. Go over the ditch in front, and forward to a stile and hunter's gate at the left edge of Hell Hole Wood. Cross the stile and go up the slope on the edge of the woodland to cross the field ahead between two pools – with attendant oak trees – to reach a gate. Go through the gate and follow a line of oaks to another gate. Go through this, and follow the left hedge to a lane. Walk right along the lane to Shelmore Large, and there follow the public bridleway (signed at the right of the cottage) along a concrete track. When the concrete goes right, continue forward on the bridleway. Follow the edge of Shelmore Wood to reach a bend on a minor road.

3 Turn left along the road, and through the bridge under the canal. Turn right up the embankment to reach the towpath, and turn right again to follow this elevated canal path for 2 miles. Arriving at a third bridge that carries the old railway bed, take the

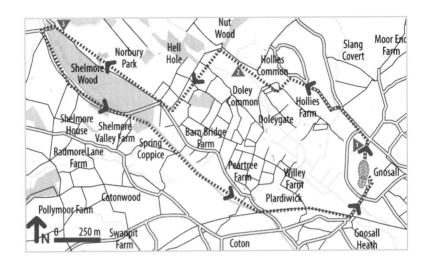

steps up and then left over the bridge, and follow the old railway for ½ mile. Leave the railway by turning right to a gate on to the A518. Go left along the pavement to the High Street through Gnosall, and so back to Knightly Road.

Points of interest

It was a long struggle to build the great embankment, involving the moving of millions of tons of earth; whilst being built it constantly slipped and collapsed. In all it took 5½ years to construct.

Ramshorn and Weaver Hill

Start At a side road in Ramshorn village, S10 3BY, GR 084453

Distance 6 miles (9.5km)

Summary Moderate

Maps OS Landranger 128

Where to eat and drink Nothing on route

A walk for a clear day when there are panoramic views over Staffordshire and neighbouring counties.

1 Go along the road towards Leek for about 300yd to a squeezer stile in a stone wall on the right just before a farm. Cross the stile and follow the path across the front of the farm. Cross a stile into a field, and follow the hedge on your right to a second stile. Cross into a third field, and go across its right corner to a fourth field. Follow the hedge to the right, and then go through to other fields to reach a farm track, on the left, which leads to a derelict farm.

2 Cross the track just short of the farm, and go through an old farm gate into a field. Go straight across to a gate in the next field, and turn right to go through a gate in the middle of a fence. Go downhill to a stile in the fence opposite. Cross the stile and go up a steep embankment, watching out for short wooden stakes directly across your path.

3 When you come to these stakes, turn right, and follow them to reach a clay track between two quarries. Cross the track to reach a stile in a fence. Cross the stile and go down an embankment to a stone wall. Follow the wall along to the right until you see a stile in the bottom corner ahead: cross the stile into a field with woods on the right. Follow the fence beside the wood to the end of this big field to reach a stile. Cross into the next field.

4 Go diagonally left uphill to a stile in the middle of the fence. Cross into the next field, still going uphill, and veer to the left, rounding the corner of the wall on the left. Go over a stile further

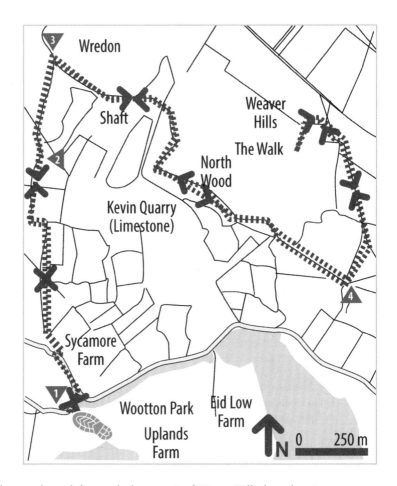

along, and turn left towards the summit of Weaver Hill where there is a stone obelisk trig point.

Another summit can be reached quite easily by returning back beyond the stile, going to the bottom right corner of the field and turning right on to a path which follows along the edge of two fields. In the third field veer right to the hilltop.

To return, go back downhill, then bear left through Kevin Quarry and back to the village of Ramshorn.

Shareshill and Laches

Start The church in Shareshill,
WV10 7LA, GR 944066

Distance 6½ miles (10.5km)

Summary Easy

Maps OS Landranger 127

Where to eat and drink The Elms,
Sharehill T01922 415380; The
Wheatsheaf, Shareshill T01922
412304

1 Pass to the left of the tower and go down through the churchyard,
and then across two fields and two stiles on to a narrow surfaced lane.
Follow the lane left to the junction opposite Lower Latherford Farm.

2 Here a right turn will take you along a lane for about a mile, passing
a marina on the left as you go; you will reach a T-junction. Turn left,
signed Four Ashes and Brewood; after ¼ mile go left, and walk to Moll's
bridge and the canal.

3 Turn left along the towpath and follow it, passing Moat House
Bridge and Laches Bridge to eventually reach Slade Heath.

4 Go under the bridge and up to the road. Turn right and take the first
left to go under the railway bridge, after which turn left, to follow a lane
to Upper Laches Farm.

5 Turn right, through the farmyard to a hunter's gate. Go through,
and follow the field edge to a gap in the fence ahead: go through this.
Follow the line of telegraph poles to Far Laches Farm, and turn left to
follow a track round the farm and down to cross a stream. Proceed along
the track a little further until you come to a wooden platform/bridge on
the left with a gate.

6 Go through the gate, and head over to the far left hedge of the field.
Follow this, then the path follows to the left of a fence to a gate, and on to
a lane. Turn left and then right to get back to the village and the church
where you started.

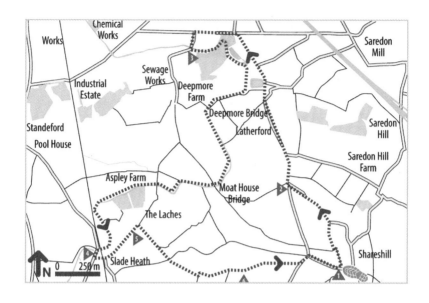

Start **The community hall car park,
ST14 5HB, GR 099407**

Distance **6 miles (9.5km)**

Summary **Fairly easy, but with one
short, steep hill**

Maps **OS Landranger 128**

Where to eat and drink **The Tavern,
Denstone, www.thetaverndenstone.
co.uk, T01889 590847; also
Denstone Hall farm shop and café,
www.denstonehall.co.uk, T01889
590050, 8.30am–4.30pm Tues–
Sat, 10.00am–4pm Sun, lunch 12
noon–3pm**

This is a circular walk from Denstone village.

[1] Go right from the car park along the road towards the B5031
and turn left on to the start of the Churnet Valley path, a dismantled
railway route. Keep on the path for approximately 2 miles, then look
out for a footbridge over the river to the left.

[2] Cross the bridge into a field and turn right. Veer left, following
a worn footpath to a stile in the left corner. Cross on to a farm track,
and go right for a few paces to a path on the left going diagonally
up a bank through trees. Go over the stile at the top into a big field
and turn right. Veer left to a gate in the top corner of the field, and
go through on to Castle Hill Road in Alton. Go past a farm and
continue downhill.

[3] Near the bottom, at a minor crossroads, you can make a
diversion by turning right to reach St John's Prep School and the
site of Alton Castle; you can also look over the wall to the Churnet
Valley below. Resume the walk by returning to the crossroads and
going straight across to Castle Road, passing St Peter's Church on
your right. This brings you to High Street. Go straight across by the
war memorial and up the path on its right, passing a cemetery and
coming out on to Hurstone Lane. Cross this road to a stile just to
the right, and cross into the bottom right corner of a large field. Go
diagonally across to a gate in the top left corner, and go through into
another large field. Go diagonally left and downhill to a stile close to

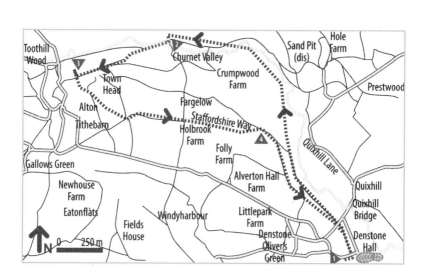

the bottom left corner. Cross the stile on to Saltersford Lane (a green lane), which is an old packhorse route used to move salt. Turn left along the lane for ¾ mile, to where it finishes at a stile.

④ Cross into a field and follow the hedge on the right to a stile. Cross and follow the waymarked signs, keeping to the hedge on the right until it turns a corner. At that point, head across the open field to the fenced woodland on the left, and follow the fence to a stile in the top left corner. Cross this stile, a bridge, and a second stile. Follow a path, keeping to the hedges on the left; just before steps up to the B5032, you reach a stile on the left. Cross this stile to return to the Churnet Valley path, and turn right to follow it back to its start, where you turn right up the road to return to the car park.

Abbots Castle and Trysull

START The layby at the end of Abbots Castle Hill, WV5 7AX, GR 835930

DISTANCE 6 miles (9.5km)

SUMMARY Easy, but you will need perseverance to follow the route in the early section of the walk

MAPS OS Landranger 138

WHERE TO EAT AND DRINK There is a selection of pubs in Trysull

A classic example of footpath loss due to lack of use and neglect. Help reverse the trend!

[1] Leave the layby and turn left along the road as far as a footpath sign for Trysull. Here turn left and cross a field to arrive at a green lane. Turn right as far as the entrance to Clan Park Farm. Turn up the farm drive, and shortly bear right behind some interesting farm buildings. Keeping to an anti-clockwise direction, follow the farm road to a point where it turns sharp right to join the road you left earlier. At the bend continue straight ahead and follow a line of telegraph poles that once, perhaps, indicated a field boundary. Coming to a hedge, keep this on your right to join, and cross, a road to a gate opposite. Through the gate and upwards brings you on to a short stretch of the Swindon Golf Course. Ahead are trees with a track through them, which soon brings you on to the open part of the golf course – beware the hazard of flying balls. For some way now the path is totally obliterated by the golf club, so make your way to the club road and the fence at the end of the driving range.

[2] Turn left to follow the fence as far as the edge of a disused quarry. Turn left again at a course sign, and then right to a point where the path is again blocked. Go over the fence and left to meet a hedge. Go right to two brick barns. Passing to the left of these, go to the end of the field and turn right for a few yards, and then left through the hedge to follow the left-hand side of the hedge ahead to meet a road on a bend. Cross the road and take the footpath signed on the left; you will shortly go over a stile, then follow the right-hand hedge to another stile and a road. Take the green lane opposite, and follow it for 1 mile to meet a road near the

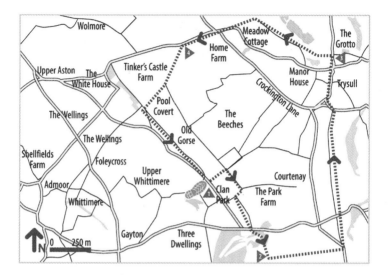

sports field. Turn left along the road, and pass the attractive Trysull village green on the left. At the road junction turn right, and walk to the crossroads by the church: go right and immediately left.

3 Shortly after crossing a bridge over Smestow Brook, turn left along the drive to the Mill House. This soon becomes a green lane to the outskirts of Seisdon. Turn left at the road, and follow it a good way almost as far as a bungalow at Little Round Hill, where on the left is an unsurfaced lane.

4 Turn up this, and follow it up on to Abbots Castle Hill escarpment. Turn left, and a short walk along the path brings you back to the start.

Points of interest

Trysull – probably owes its name to the Tresel, an ancient name for Smestow Brook.

Abbots Castle Hill – the ridge path offers views across the Shropshire lowlands to the Clee Hills and Wenlock Edge.

59 Kingsley and Booth's Hall

Start The church of St Werburgh, Kingsley, ST10 2AA, GR 009471

Distance 6 miles (9.5km)

Summary Steep descents and ascents in and out of the valley twice, but otherwise easy

Maps OS Landranger 119

Where to eat and drink Fox and Goose, Foxt To1538 266415

A fascinating trip into a hidden valley. Good for nature lovers and tree buffs.

① Go through the churchyard past the tower, and diagonally left over two stiles into a field. Go left along the field and over a stile. Go diagonally right across an open field, and exit through a squeezer in the top left corner. Continue on the same line to a stile in the corner; go over, and straight ahead to trees and another stile. Cross this, and follow the path down through trees to cross a lane. Go over a stile and down to the River Churnet. Go under the railway bridge and right over a footbridge, and up to the Caldon canal. Turn left here to Cherryeye bridge, and cross it. Turn diagonally right across a field towards a wood. Follow the path up through the woods to the top, go over a stile and cross the small field to another stile.

② Do not go through the stile, but turn left and follow the field boundary to a gate into another field. Follow the wall on the right, but when it turns right, go straight on to the woods, and take a wide track going down to a stream. Cross a stile and footbridge, and go up steps to a stile. Cross into a field and go uphill to the top corner near Booth's Wood farm and out over a fence. Pass the farm on its right and go over stiles to pass Booth's Hall. Start along the farm lane, but almost immediately go over a stile on the left and diagonally across the field to the second gate on the left from the farm lane. Go diagonally left to the far field corner, straight across to two stiles, then over to the far left corner, a squeezer and the road.

③ Turn left, and follow the road past an S-bend. At the next wood, turn left down a footpath marked to Consall Forge. Go over a stream and up steps to a lane. Go left for 50yd to squeezers, and then follow the field edge, going slightly into the woods and then down the Devil's Staircase.

④ At the bottom you reach the Black Lion pub; cross in front of it to reach the Caldon canal. Go left along the canal towpath to the Flint Mill. Cross the canal here and go over the railway and the River Churnet.

⑤ Then go upwards through the nature reserve. When you meet the road, turn left for a few hundred yards and go left again by a letterbox. After 50yd go right through a gate and across fields to eventually reach the church and starting point.

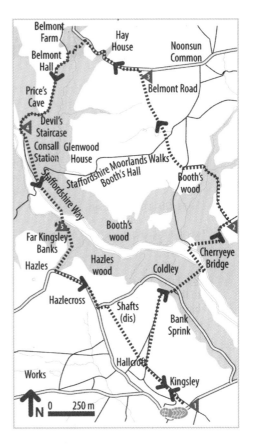

Points of interest

Caldon canal is a 17-mile canal completed in 1777 to carry limestone from Caldon quarries to the Trent and Mersey canal at Stoke-on-Trent. It is now a popular leisure canal.

Flint Mill was erected by John Leigh, Lord of the Manor, in the 1830s to grind Australian sand and pebbles into glaze for the pottery industry.

START **Deep Hayes Country Park car park, ST13 7JS, GR 960533**

DISTANCE **6 miles (9.5km)**

SUMMARY **Easy**

MAPS **OS Landranger 118**

WHERE TO EAT AND DRINK **The Hollybush Inn, Denford, www. hollybushinn-denford.co.uk, T01538 371 819, Mon–Fri 11.00am–11.00pm, Sun 12.00pm–11.00pm, food is served 12.00pm–8.30pm every day. Also The Wheel Inn, Longsdon, T01538 385012**

A fairly easy walk, with interesting valley, hill and woodland scenery.

1 From the car park, go back out of the entrance and down left on to the Caldon canal. Follow it west until the junction with the Leek branch of the canal.

2 Here, cross the footbridge on to the Leek branch and return in the same direction, with the main waterway below. Continue along this canal, crossing over the Caldon canal, to reach the Leek tunnel. Take the path over the top of this, and negotiate the stiles and drop-down to the canal towpath again at the far side of the tunnel.

3 At the end of the canal carry straight on, along the canal feeder and over a stile. Where the canal feeder passes under an unfenced farm lane, turn right on to the lane to reach the busy A53. Cross the road and take the track on the left of the feeder to pass to the right of a council depot. At the end of the depot, bend left around the back of it and follow the path, which is waymarked with numerous walks; continue, keeping the boundary on your left.

4 After a number of the coloured walks have gone off to the left, walk up towards the woods and bear slightly to the right to cross a stile into the woods. Pass through the wood and out into open fields, and turn right on to a track shortly afterwards. Follow this across a minor road, through a field and over a stile on to the A53. Turn right along the A53, and then left down Sutherland Road

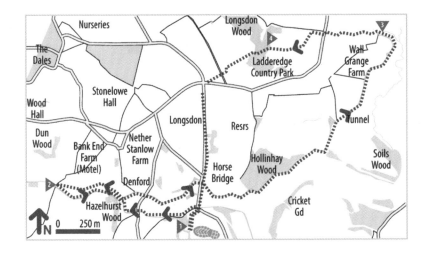

shortly afterwards. Pass over a canal and the railway, and turn right into the entrance to Deep Hayes Country Park car park.

Start The Alstonefield car park with public toilets, DE6 2FY, GR 131557

Distance 6½ miles (10.5km)

Summary Easy

Maps OS Landranger 119

Where to eat and drink The George in Alstonefield, www. thegeorgeatalstonefield.com, T01335 310 205, Mon–Thurs 11.30am–3pm and 6pm–11pm, Fri and Sat 11.30am–11pm, Sun 12pm–9.30pm; food times vary

A fairly easy walk from a very pretty village.

① Leave the car park and turn left along the road. Keep left around the bend: pass the first track on the left, and take the second track on the left to pass the youth hostel. Follow this track for about a mile until you reach a stile, and go over it: there is a steep descent to the River Dove.

② Cross the bridge at the bottom, and go right along the riverside path; after a mile you reach a road. Go left on the road for about a quarter of a mile to a signposted path on the right. The path starts steeply, but it is only a short way to the fields above. At the top go right over a stile on to a path that goes along the wall, crossing four fields, and then descends steeply to the river at a footbridge at Milldale. Keep this side of the river and follow the path beside the water for about 1¼ miles, passing Dove Holes (caves) as you go.

③ You will come to a footbridge near Ilam Rock. Cross this bridge and turn right to follow the river upstream this time. The path goes left up Hall Dale; at the top cross the stile into a field, where the path veers right to cross two more stiles on to a rough track by a footpath sign. Turn left to reach a road.

④ Turn right on the road, then right on the track between Stanshope Hall and the farm. Continue and descend to the road in Hope Dale. Cross to a stile opposite, and continue steeply up the hillside, swinging left at the top; follow the boundary wall to a stile and gate. Over the stile keep straight ahead, turning right at the road back into Alstonefield. Navigate through the village by keeping right, but then take the left fork and left again to regain the car park at the start.

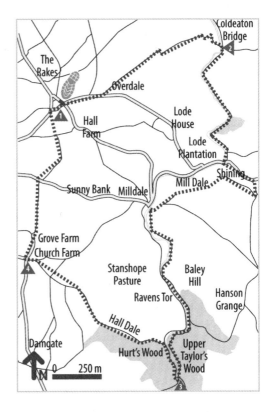

Points of interest

Milldale is the packhorse bridge, known as Viator's Bridge; it is referred to in the 1676 edition of Izaak Walton's *Compleat Angler*.

Alstonefield was originally a Saxon settlement, and once a busy market town – its charter was granted in 1308 – and the crossroads of several packhorse ways. The church is the third on the same site and has a Norman south doorway, a chancel arch and fine seventeenth-century pews.

Oakamoor and Hawksmoor Woods

START The Churnet Valley car park, Oakamoor, ST10 3AG, GR 053446

DISTANCE 6½ miles (10.5km)

SUMMARY Moderate

MAPS OS Landranger 128

WHERE TO EAT AND DRINK The Ramblers Retreat (To1538 702730).www. ramblersretreat.co.uk, Mar–Oct: Mon–Fri 10am–5pm, weekends 10am–6pm; Nov–Feb: Mon–Fri 10.30am–3pm, weekends 10am–5pm

A lovely walk through wooded dales and by streams and brooks.

1 Facing the car park entrance, go to the stile in the top left corner, and over it on to the road. Turn left and go to the road junction, and turn right on to Stony Dale road, going uphill. After about ½ mile, turn off right on to a woodland track with a log barrier across, and go uphill through the trees. At the top branch right, and follow the track down to a road, reaching a bungalow.

2 Turn left up the road, and after 200yd you will see the stone pillars of Hawksmoor Nature Reserve on the right. Go through the gate, and take the track to the right going downhill. At a junction with another track turn left, and then cross a stile on the left of a brick wall. Eastwall Farm is down on the right. Ignore the stile in the corner, and follow a path that bears left and runs around the hill and then goes along the edge of Gibbridding Wood.

3 Go up out of a gully and right through a kissing gate. With the wood on your right, follow the path as it snake bends up to the right and through fields and a pedestrian gate, to eventually reach a lane. Turn left and go for half a mile along the road, turn right at a junction, and shortly left to Highshutt Farm.

4 Go through the farm, and veer left on to a path going along the right edge of two fields. In the third field bear left to a gate, and in the fourth field go to the right corner, and over a wood bar fence on to a lane. Turn right, and at the T-junction in the hamlet of Old

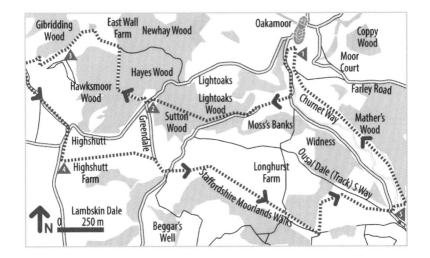

Furnace go straight across to a lane left of the house. Keep on this lane until a fishpond is seen on the right. Turn right at the end of the path at a second fishpond. When you come to a wide track, turn left along this and go for another ¼ mile, to arrive at the side of Ramblers Retreat coffee house.

⑤ Cross the road that runs in front of the café, and follow a path over a river bridge and railway bridge. Turn left and down to Churnet Valley Railway path. Turn right for about 1½ miles to cross a stile, and follow this path back to a log bar. Cross this, and follow a track to a pedestrian bridge on the left over the river. Cross the bridge and make your way back to the car park.

Points of interest

Hawksmoor Nature Reserve is a fine reserve created during the late 1920s at the suggestion of J. R. B. Masefield. A plaque at the main entrance gate records his keen interest and great love for the natural history of the area.

63 The Manifold Way

START **Waterhouses old station car park, ST10 3EG, GR 085501**

DISTANCE **6½ miles (10.5km)**

SUMMARY **Easy**

MAPS **OS Landranger 119**

WHERE TO EAT AND DRINK **Ye Old Crown Inn at Waterhouses, T01538 308 204**

A straightforward walk through interesting country.

① Descend a tarmac ramp to the road following a marked cycle lane across and to the start of the Manifold Way track. Follow this down the valley criss-crossing the River Hamps for approximately 3¼ miles to the junction with the Manifold Valley, where the track swings left. The limestone cliff of Beeston Tor is over on the far side of the valley.

② Turn right off the track and across fields towards a bridge. Cross the bridge and stile, and follow the track towards a farm. Just before the farm, fork right up a gradient, passing through a gate and over a stile as the track bends away from the valley. Soon you will be approaching a wall: head for a right-angled corner on the left, and pass between a copse on the left and the continuing wall on the right. Go through a gate where the wall crosses the path. Leave the copse on the left, and pass through a second gate. Bear right, and then as Soles Hill comes into view across the valley ahead, bear left and walk parallel to and above the valley, heading south. Aim for a copse and a road in the distance. On striking the road, turn right and continue, passing three farm tracks on the right.

③ After about 500yd, shortly beyond a farm on the right at Farwall, turn right down a track. Then after about 650yd, go over a stone stile on the right – it is easily missed. Go over a second stile ahead, but just before a third stile, turn right, and follow this path as it descends into the Hamps Valley and reaches the Manifold Way track. Turn left to the main road at Waterhouses, and return to the car park.

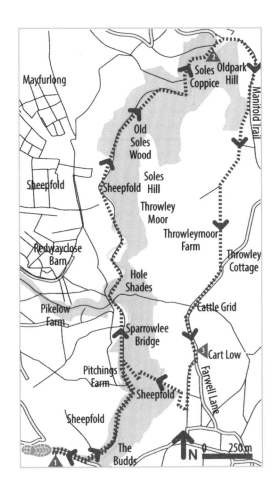

Points of interest

The Hamps Valley is deeply incised, often with a dry riverbed, and contains a variety of beautiful spring flowers: these should not be picked.

Beeston Tor is well known for its climbers.

Alton and the Churnet Valley

START Townhead Farm on the edge of Alton, ST10 4AJ, GR 075426

DISTANCE 6½ miles (10.5km)

SUMMARY Moderate

MAPS OS Landranger 119

WHERE TO EAT AND DRINK There is a selection of pubs in the village of Alton, in particular The Blacksmith Arms www.blacksmithsarmsalton. co.uk, T01538 702111, and Alton Bridge Hotel www.altonbridgehotel. co.uk/

A varied and interesting walk.

1 Go into the fields with the farm buildings on your left. As you cross the field, veer towards the stone wall on your left; a stone stile in this leads into the woodlands overlooking the Churnet Valley – the path zigzags down to the bottom. Cross the farm track into the field, which leads down to the River Churnet and the footbridge across it. Go over the bridge into a flat field, and walk for about ¼ mile to a gate. Go through and across a track, and through another gate. Follow the canal towpath for a short distance until you reach the old packhorse bridge. Go over it, and up the field and into the woodland. Follow the path through the wood to join a track. After a short distance the route bends round to the right, and then crosses a field.

2 Go down through more woodland, to come out by the side of the lake. Bear off left, walking along past Brookley, go over the bridge and then off left to join a lane.

3 Turn left towards Farley and follow the lane for 1½ miles to the village. At the junction in Farley walk on in the direction of Cotton and Oakamoor.

4 You will reach a stile on the left: go over this, and follow a path through fields until you reach the rear of an old lodge on a road. Do not go out on to the road, but turn right on a track that leads down Barberry Dale. Not far down the track you will see an ancient and

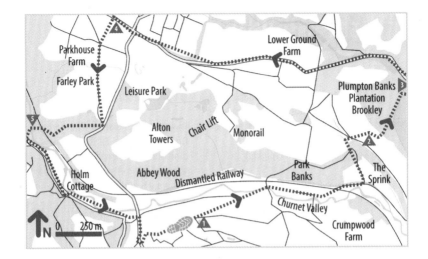

massive oak tree, which is said to have associations with Druids.
Follow the route down Barberry Dale and go over the bridge that
spans the old rail track.

5 Then go over the bridge that spans the River Churnet, and soon
you come to the road and the Ramblers Retreat. Go left to take
the road to Alton. Turn right up the steep hill, and as you come to
buildings on the left, look for a footpath off to the left. Take this
uphill past the side of the church on to the road; go straight on up to
Townhead Farm.

Points of interest

Alton Castle was designed by Pugin and erected for the Earl of
Shrewsbury. The present castle was built during the 1830s and
1840s, and occupies the site of two earlier castles.

START The small car park behind the parish hall opposite the church, DE6 2HB, GR 116435

DISTANCE 6½ miles (10.5km)

SUMMARY Easy, but with some steep sections

MAPS OS Landranger 119

WHERE TO EAT AND DRINK The Duncombe Arms, Ellastone, www.duncombearms.co.uk/, (T 01335 324275), Mon–Thurs 12–2.30pm and 6–9pm, Fri and Sat 12–2.30pm and 5.30–10pm, Sun 12–8pm

A fine circular walk from Ellastone.

1   Turn left up Church Lane. After 300yd go right at a footpath sign into a field. Go left of the farm down to a stile; the route follows yellow arrow waymarkers across stiles and footbridges uphill to reach a gate in an iron fence at Wootton Hall Farm. Go through and across the paddock to a stile on the right of the farm, and on to a track. Turn right and join Hall Lane.

2   Pass a house where a track goes off right: there is a stile in the wall. Cross this, and go diagonally right up to a stile in the hedge. Cross it, and go straight across the field to a wooden stile, which you also cross; continue to the top left corner to another wooden stile and gateway beyond. Go through, then diagonally left to a gate. Go through, then keep to the right hedge and go steeply down to find a stile at the bottom. Cross the brook, then go right and then left up the slope, and right to a gateway on the left.

3   Go through the gateway, then veer to the left of a middle hedge, and over to the far opposite corner. Cross the stile and continue along a narrow section; eventually you will pick up a track that passes a dwelling. In a few yards you will see a stile on the right in a stone wall: go through this, cross a small brook, then go uphill through a stile in a wall to another, and so access a small lane.

4   Turn right into Stanton village and right again. Go left and leave the village along Sallyfield Lane. Downhill beyond the hairpin

take a signposted footpath on the right to a green lane. Follow this through a gate to a woodland path.

⑤ After crossing a small streamlet, a small post waymarks the crossing of footpaths. Turn left down to a footbridge, and follow the path up the other side to cross a wooden stile. Go straight uphill to a stile in the top hedge. Cross this and turn right.

⑥ The route then follows the waymarked path across stiles and through gates, passing close to Ashfield Farm and eventually Hutts Farm, which you leave through a gate. Go across the middle of the field beyond to a stile at the far side.

⑦ Cross and follow the green path, but veer off to the right and eventually down to a stile and footbridge over the brook.

⑧ Follow the yellow arrow waymarkers around the right of the farm to emerge on to the road. Turn left, and just after the farm take the stile on the right. Cross and go diagonally right to a stile and footbridge under trees. Continue along a similar line across more fields and stiles before heading diagonally right to a kissing gate in the churchyard wall. Go through and follow the path to the left to rejoin the start.

Hilderstone and Leigh

Start The junction of Hill Lane and Bustomley Lane between the hamlets of Middleton Green and Merrilow Heath, GR 987351

Distance 6¾ miles (10.8km)

Summary Easy

Maps OS Landranger 127

Where to eat and drink Nothing on route

A walk through fields and along typical old English lanes.

1 Walk along Hill Lane to Middleton Green, and turn left down Leigh Lane. At the T-junction enter the fields opposite and follow the footpath, which leads past Daisy House Farm. From the farm the route follows the farm track for about ¼ mile in a north-westerly direction.

2 The route then turns left up the fields, passing alongside the remains of a large moat; just after Bitternsdale you join Bustomley Lane, where you turn right. In less than 1 mile you will arrive at the starting point: here, straight over the crossroads in the direction of Garshall Green. At the next crossroads turn left along the lane, and at the next junction turn left again, and continue a short way.

3 Turn left on a path to go through fields. Follow the footpath past Sherratts Wood, and you will soon reach Hill Lane; here turn left, and in a short distance you come back to the starting point.

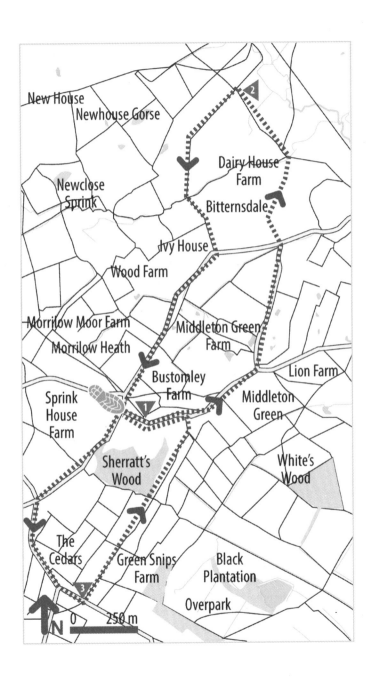

New House
Newhouse Gorse

Newclose
Sprink

Dairy House
Farm

Bitternsdale

Ivy House

Wood Farm

Morrilow Moor Farm

Middleton Green
Farm

Morrilow Heath

Bustomley
Farm

Lion Farm

Sprink
House
Farm

Middleton
Green

Sherratt's
Wood

White's
Wood

The
Cedars

Green Snips
Farm

Black
Plantation

Overpark

0   250 m

N

Middle Mayfield and Standlow

Start On the roadside near Old Hall Farm, DE6 2JU, GR 147449

Distance 7 miles (11.2km)

Summary Moderate

Maps OS Landranger 119

Where to eat and drink Nothing on route

A relatively easy walk with fine scenic views.

[1] From the three-fingered signpost go up the narrow track a few yards, then right over a stile. Ascend the field, swinging right to follow the boundary hedge, and cross two more fields to reach a stile in the facing hedge. Do not cross this, but turn right along a clear track passing through several gateways to reach Stanton Lane. Cross the lane and stile opposite (by the gate post), and keep ahead past Lordspiece Farm to a gate. Go through this, and across two fields by clearly seen stiles, and follow the right boundary over the next four fields to a stile where the hedge turns a corner. Cross this stile, and another on the left near a tree, to continue up the field and through a gateway as far as a wall stile on the right.

[2] Do not cross this, but turn left and then go through a gateway and around Newhouse farmyard to a drive on the far side. Turn right over a cattlegrid, then left into a field. Follow the drive side wall through a gate. Cross the next two fields using stiles, and continue across the following fields through gates to reach a farm. Here turn left to pass between the buildings, and go straight ahead over a stile to follow first the boundary fence, then a distinct path over the hilltop: from here there are wide-ranging views. Turn right by the sheep wire fence at the top of Cuckoo Cliff, and down to a stile: having crossed, you will find yourself at the top of a steep flight of steps – negotiate these with care, and use the handrail. The steps descend into the wooded ravine of the Ellis Hill brook: cross over the brook on the footbridge, on to a short path with a stile. Go directly up the hillside – there may be no path line – through the line of trees, and then bear right to follow a line parallel to the hedge: you will reach a gate in the corner, with a lane beyond.

③ Follow the lane to its junction with the road through Stanton village. Turn left, then right at a barn on to Honeywall Lane. After the fork to a farm lane the route becomes a track, which eventually ends at a field boundary. Continue straight ahead on a grassy way between walls (the right-hand one is broken down); this leads to an open area, and then there is a clear path through trees to a stile at the edge of the wood. Descend the slightly hollow way through the wood, and cross a stile at the far side. Turn right on to a grassy path, and follow this down.

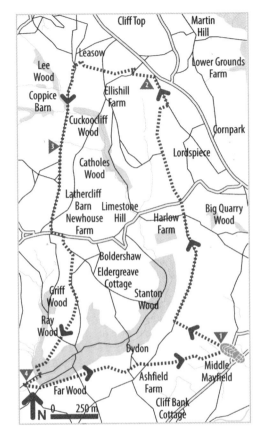

④ At the bottom go left, and cross the footbridge over Ordley Brook. Ascend the field to cross a stile by the wall corner, continuing left along the boundary to cross two more stiles. Bear right to a hedge corner, going along the hillside to another corner. Follow the hedge and wall to a stile. Go over this and a similar one in the next corner, and then cross diagonally to a gate. Turn left across a farm drive, and go through another gate before bearing right to cross a stile. Go left through another gate, then diagonally right across a small fence stile to a stile in the far corner. Cross this, and continue ahead through a gap in trees and over a stile – this may be obscured from view by holly trees in the next field corner. On the same line, cross the next corner stile, before turning down the field to a gate hidden by trees. Go through this, and turn left down the hollow lane back to the starting point.

68 Weeford

Start On the roadside verge opposite Weeford Church, WS14 0PW, GR 141039

Distance 7 miles (11.2km)

Summary Easy

Maps OS Landranger 139

Where to eat and drink Old School House Restaurant T01543 480009; Holly Bush in Lichfield T01543 481217

This walk takes in much of the Canwell estate.

[1] From the church go up the road to the Schoolhouse Restaurant, turn right through the car park and continue along a broad track. Go over a stile, and continue walking with the hedge, then a wall, on your right; you will arrive at another stile to the drive of Bourne House cottage. Cross the drive and go over the stile opposite to arrive at another drive; here you turn right, then fork left on to an unsurfaced lane that crosses the Black Brook. Pass to the left of an industrial unit, and up to the first oak tree in the hedge on the left. Go over the wooden stile on the left, and cross the field with the fence on your left, to a stile into Job's Hill Plantation. Follow the edge of the plantation and the next field to join a narrow lane. Turn right, and keep going for a little over a mile to Brockhurst Farm.

[2] Just past the farm go through the metal stile on the right and over the field beyond to a wooden stile. Cross this, and keeping left of trees, follow a similar line across more stiles, a drive and fields to enter Weeford Park Plantation. Follow a wide track through to the busy A38. Cross to a stile opposite. Go over the stile and follow the path through the plantation, and join the farm lane near a bridge over the motorway. Go over the bridge; the route then passes farm buildings and goes into fields – continue with the hedge on your left. You will reach a gate and stile: cross these on to a track at the side of a covert. Go past Pine Tree Cottage to a road, and turn right. Continue along this road for about ⅓ mile.

[3] You will come to a signed footpath on the right (opposite a stand of trees): take this across the field, and over a stile and overgrown footbridge. Continue with a hedge on your right to a gate on to the

corner of a lane.
Go along the lane
for a few yards,
and take the
signed bridleway
to the right, to
reach a metal
hunter's gate. Go
through this, and
turn left along
the right fence
and wood edge
to a gate on to a
green lane. This
broadens to a wide,
unsurfaced lane
near a bungalow.
Continue for ¾

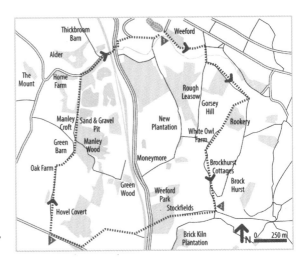

mile to a metalled road, and turn right to reach the A38. Go over the
main road by using the footbridge on the left, and as you descend on the
other side take a signposted footpath beyond the wooden fences on the
right. Cross the field over the brow heading towards the building which
is just visible. Cross the stile and yard of the building, and join a lane
where you turn right for Weeford Church.

Points of interest

This walk is mostly on the Canwell estate, an attractive mix of
rolling woodland and pastures. Many centuries ago it was part
of the Benedictine Priory estates of Canwell, which then came
under the patronage of the Bassetts family. However, as a result of the Battle
of Evesham in 1265 the family line became extinct, so the estate passed
through several families over the succeeding centuries – it was also owned
at one stage by the City of Birmingham, to provide land for war veterans.

Leek and Morridge

Start Just off the Leek to Ashbourne road, GR 997556

Distance 7 miles (11.2km)

Summary Moderate/Demanding

Maps OS Landranger 118 and 119

Where to eat and drink Leek has plenty of good pubs and a selection of cafés and tearooms

A demanding walk with some steep climbs, but with excellent views across the western Peak District.

1 Go past the T-junction and round a right-hand bend to cross a bridge over the main road. Go down and pass Home Farm, and follow a surfaced track to where it bends right. Here, go left over a wooden stile next to a gate and down to the left (east) corner of the field. Follow the field boundary and bear right through the next boundary into the valley bottom. Cross the railway and go up through a wooded area. Climb up and out of this, and follow a lane left. Shortly take a right fork, and the old Ashenhurst Mill, now a private residence, soon comes into view.

2 Once alongside the mill, bear off right, away from the main track and along a green lane. Follow this across fields to reach a well-made road which leads to the Egg Well. Go to the left of a bungalow, and follow a lane up to a gate. Go through, and take an S-shape route through the field to join an ancient roadway. Follow this and join a farm track, which soon curves round to the right.

3 Just before you start to come out of the curve, go left over a stile to cross fields in a north-easterly direction. Avoid the gate at a stream and cross it a little to the right to find a stile in the corner. Continue across fields to the railway, and the main Leek to Ashbourne road beyond. Opposite and a little to the right is Cooks Lane: take this up to a farm: as you approach the yard bear right, then almost straightaway turn left, and follow the lane up to where it becomes concreted. After the concrete section finishes, go over a stile by a gate, and then another stile, and follow the wall on your left. After a short distance go over a stile in this wall next to a gate, and cross fields and more stiles to reach a barn near

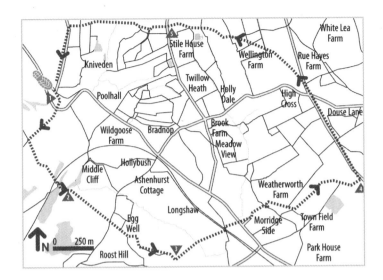

a wind turbine. Pass the barn following a farm track to its right, and continue on this track up to the road and Morridge.

④ Go left at the road junction, and just beyond take a turn left over stiles and across fields above Wellington Farm heading for Bealey Barn. Continue pass this to Stile House Farm, which you pass on the right.

⑤ Just after, cross a lane and go over a stile, and down a field to Holly House. Go through another stile, and follow waymarks as directed to go steeply down, across a stream and then up fields to meet a narrow pathway between high walls near a large health property. On reaching the road, turn left to return to the start.

Points of interest

Egg Well is an ancient well said to have been used by the Romans; it is said to have healing properties.

Leek is a well-preserved town with splendid Victorian buildings. It has a fascinating industrial heritage, and a visit to the Brindley Water Mill is well worthwhile.

Wetton Mill, Butterton and Warslow

START The car park in Wetton Mill, DE6 2AG, GR 095561

MAPS OS Landranger 119

DISTANCE 7 miles (11.2km)

WHERE TO EAT AND DRINK The tea room at Wetton Mill, during the season

SUMMARY Moderate

A pleasant walk with a variety of scenery.

1 From the car park, cross the road and pass through a gate on to a wide path; 300yd further on it follows alongside Hoo Brook to the junction of five footpaths. Take the one veering right, still on the right-hand bank of the brook, but crossing to the left after approximately 400yd. Continue along the brook to where the path ends, and there turn left up the field to a gate and the road into Butterton.

2 Follow the road through the village, keeping right at the junction to pass The Black Lion inn; you will reach a junction adjacent to the church. Turn right, then left along a walled track, and where it ends, continue in a straight line down the field to cross the brook and the stile opposite. Occasionally the brook may be too high to ford, in which case go left along it, swinging left up the field to a small gate in the roadside wall, then follow the road up to a T-junction. If you can ford the brook, then climb the field to cross a stile near the left corner on to the road near the T-junction.

3 Go left on the minor road, turning right over a nearby stile, and follow the boundary to a second stile. Cross to find a third at a footpath crossroads. Go over the stile and follow the field boundary as it swings left before reaching a rough track. Follow this through to the road at Warslow. Go down through the village to a road junction. Turn left, then go right over the road to a stile adjacent to a farmhouse. Cross this, and the one opposite, and continue along the left boundary to a stile in the corner. Cross this, and follow the wall down the field. Turn through a gate and go diagonally left to a wall

stile hidden by bushes. A clear path beyond leads to the road, across which can be seen the remains of the Dale lead mine. Descend on the road to cross the River Manifold.

4 Here, turn right on to the Manifold Trail. Follow the trail for an easy and scenic walk back to Wetton Mill.

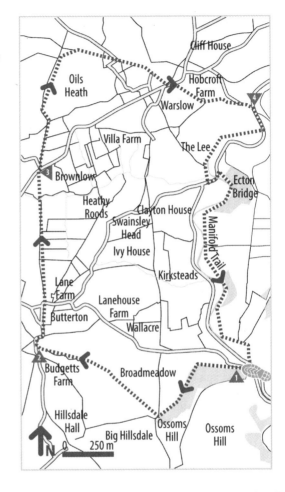

Points of interest

At Wetton Mills a nearby rock shelter contained animal remains of the late glacial period (80,000BC) and Mesolithic man. Excavations of other caves or rock shelters along the valley nearby revealed remains of man and animals spanning the period from the late Upper Paleolithic period through to the Bronze Age.

71 Cannock Chase

START Millford Common car park,
ST17 0UH, GR 972211

MAPS OS Landranger 127

DISTANCE 7 miles (11.2km)

WHERE TO EAT AND DRINK Barley Mow,
28 Main Road in Milford, T01785
665230, daily 11am–11pm

SUMMARY Moderate

A pleasant walk down to a brook with stepping stones, and then
through the forest where deer can sometimes be seen.

[1] Walk left out of the car park entrance and take the signed path
to the left up a slight rise; you will soon pass the Sister Dora Home
on the right. Keep on along the track, which curves down and joins
another track. Keep on the wide centre track, ignoring other paths
going off to the left and right. Eventually you will reach a direction
post on the left, signed for Coppice Hill and the Punch Bowl. Here,
turn left down the signed track. This joins a wider track on a bend.
Turn right on to this new track, following an old post and wire fence
on the left. Follow this down to the brook, which you cross using the
stepping stones.

[2] Take the first path off to the right. This path continues in the
same direction, but stays on the left of the brook. Continue for just
over a mile to reach a T-junction with a track.

[3] Turn left uphill on this new track; when you come to a crossing
of tracks, go straight across between pine trees. Continue straight
ahead at a second crossing of tracks, and also at a third, now going
downhill.

[4] At the bottom, turn left at a T-junction with a reddish-brown
track, and continue along this for about 1½ miles, taking the main
path through trees to Seven Springs picnic area and car park.

[5] Turn left in the car park, and take the track beyond the barrier.
At the first fork take the right path uphill, and continue along this

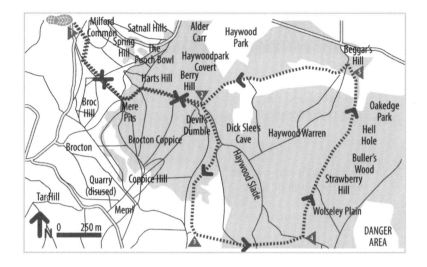

main path, ignoring any minor paths going off to the left or right. Eventually you meet a wire fence on the right, and soon get back to the stepping stones. Once across these, go right to return to the car park by reversing the outward route.

Freehay and Threapwood

START In Croxden Lane, 2 miles south-east of Cheadle, GR 029412

DISTANCE 7 miles (11.2km)

SUMMARY Fairly easy, with one moderately steep hill section

MAPS OS Landranger 119

WHERE TO EAT AND DRINK The Queens at Freehay, www.queensatfreehay. co.uk, T01538 722383

A walk down country lanes and over fields.

① Walk along Croxden Lane to a road junction, and turn right towards Greatgate.

② Just before the village there is a stone stile in the wall on the left. Go over this into a field, and take the path that ascends to higher ground. From the stone wall at the top the path crosses a field towards woodland. The path itself is not well defined, but there are stiles that assist with way finding. The walk goes through woodland and fields towards the B5032 at Threapwood. Between the woodland and the road the view to the south-east on clear days is extensive, and you can see as far as Leicestershire. As you near the B5032, the route bears right to join a minor road at Bradley Lane end.

③ Turn left on this road and join the B5032. Go left along it for about 500yd to Threapwood, where at the crossroads you turn left along the lane towards Great Gate. Follow this pleasant road (known as Sandy Lane) for 1½ miles, and finally turn right up Croxden Lane. The last section of the walk retraces the outward section.

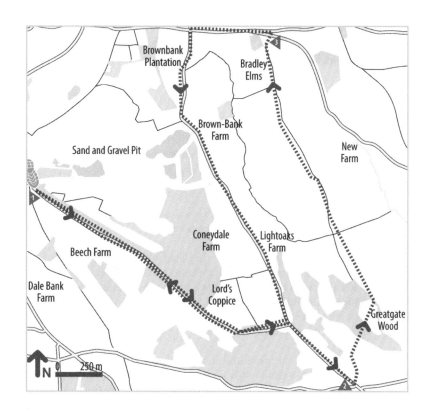

73 Penkridge and Pillaton

START The public car park in
Penkridge, ST19 5AF, GR 922140

DISTANCE 7 miles (11.2km)

SUMMARY Easy

MAPS OS Landranger 127

WHERE TO EAT AND DRINK The Boat Inn
at Penkridge, http://theboatinn.org.
uk, T01785 715 170

This walk passes under the M6 motorway twice, but soon leaves the
traffic noise behind for a wooded, rural interlude.

1 From the car park go right to the island in the village centre.
There bear right, and right again at the next junction. Follow the
road past several historic shops and hostelries to the Boat Inn on the
Staffordshire and Worcestershire Canal. Go right along the towpath
for a little more than a mile to the sixth bridge at Otherton Lock,
opposite Otherton Farm.

2 Go left over the bridge and under the motorway to a gate, and
then left across a field to a fence stile. In the next field turn right
along the edge for about 10yd, and then strike left across the field
on a bearing of 25 degrees (just left of the buildings), to arrive at a
gate on a bend in a farm drive. Go right to pass Moor Hall cottages,
and continue along the drive. At a junction turn left to pass, on your
right, the historic Pillaton Old Hall. Continue past Pillaton Hall
Farm to reach a road.

3 Turn right for a short way, then go left at the sign for the Cats
Holiday Hotel along a quiet lane to another road. Here go right, and
then left along the No Through Road, which becomes more of a track
as it swings left to Bangley Park Farm.

4 At the farmhouse the track swings right through a gate into
Hayes Wood. Follow the track along the woodland edge, and then
left to a stile in a fence. Do not cross the stile but turn right, with the
fence on your left, to another stile. Go left to a gate and stile into a
hedged green lane, which becomes a surfaced lane on joining that

from Wood Bank Farm. Continue for about 100yd, and take the track on the right, through trees, to the gate into the Teddesley estate.

⑤ Here go left and under the motorway again to join the canal and the towpath back to the Boat Inn and Penkridge.

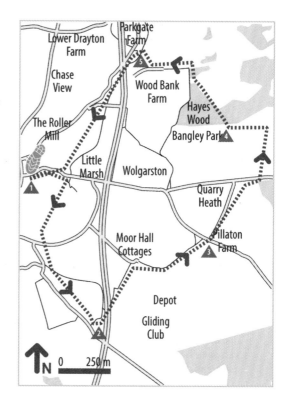

Points of interest

Penkridge is a very old market village; the cattle market has been held there since the thirteenth century.

Pillaton Old Hall was the seat of the Littleton family prior to Sir Edward Littleton building Teddesley Hall. The Old Hall is reputed to have contained a secret hoard of coins, which paid for the building of the new hall.

START By the school in Upper Hulme, GR 013609

MAPS OS Landranger 118 and 119

DISTANCE 7½ miles (12km)

SUMMARY Moderate; some sections are covered in vegetation, which makes walking difficult

WHERE TO EAT AND DRINK The Rock Inn in Upper Hulme, www.yeolderockinn.org.uk, T01538 300324; Mon–Fri from 6pm, Sat, Sun and Bank Holidays from 12 noon

An invigorating walk over some of the highest ground in Staffordshire.

Descend to the hamlet and turn right, before the stream, up a concrete lane. Follow the right bank of the stream, and cross it in front of Dains Mill ruin, then follow the left bank.

1 Just before you get to a ruined barn, turn left to a stile next to a farm gate. Go through the stile and head diagonally right following an open track to a stile alongside a field gate. Go through the stile and straight ahead over the brow, and head towards a cleft valley and trees. Go through wooden gated stiles and follow the direction shown by the yellow arrows on the gates. Cross the stream in the cleft valley, and follow the path left out of the cleft and over a wooden footbridge. Then follow the path to the right, up to Misty Hill Farm; go through a wooden gated stile and pass between the barn and farmhouse. Turn left along the driveway to reach the road, and turn left. Ignore the first road on the left and keep right, and at the next junction take a track on the right-hand side of the house.

2 Pass Newstones Rock, and follow the ridge to reach rocks with some old gritstone walls. This area is Black Brook Nature Reserve. Turn right and over the gritstone walls. The path curves left and onwards to a forest area, and eventually emerges on to a minor road.

3 Go left to a junction, then left again for just over ½ mile to a crossroads. Go left here and across the next road into a farm lane. Go down this lane and take the right branch for a farm.

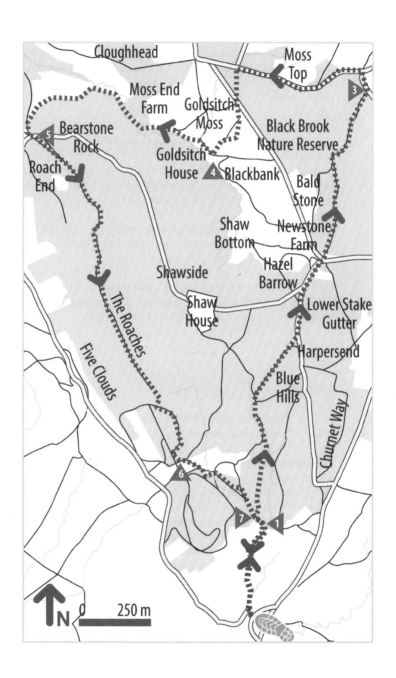

Cloughhead

Moss Top

Moss End Farm

Goldsitch Moss

3

Bearstone Rock

5

Black Brook Nature Reserve

Roach End

Goldsitch House

4

Blackbank

Bald Stone

Shaw Bottom

Newstone Farm

The Roaches

Shawside

Hazel Barrow

Five Clouds

Shaw House

Lower Stake Gutter

Harpersend

Blue Hills

Churnet Way

6

7

1

N

0   250 m

4 Just before the farm turn right and diagonally down to a stile in a corner by Black Brook. Follow the old lane on the right of the brook to a footbridge. Cross this and go up the other side, and continue until you get to a road.

5 Cross straight over to Bearstone Rock, and follow the wide path along the edge of the Roaches, passing Doxey Pool on the left. The path descends to a gap; go down to the right through the gap, and then turn left under the main tier of Rockhall Cottage. Below the cottage turn left, and follow the wall to the second stile and go over this; then immediately go diagonally left towards a farm.

6 Go over stiles and head round to the right of the farm and through another stile on to the farm road. Turn right down the track for about ⅓ mile to where it bends sharply right.

7 Here leave the track, go straight ahead along a footpath and through a stile, and in front of the ruined barn rejoin the outward section of the walk. Reverse this first section back to Upper Hulme.

Points of interest

Black Brook Nature Reserve is one of Staffordshire Wildlife Trust's largest nature reserves, and a haven for rare birds.

Rockhall Cottage (also known as the Don Whillans Hut) was once the home of Bess Bower, daughter of a Moss Trooper and now used by rock climbers. The cottage is built into the rock face and the kitchen is a cave!

Roaches, Gibb Torr and Newstones Rocks are outcrops that are justly famous for the variety and outstanding quality of their rock-climbing routes. From the Roaches skyline it is sometimes possible to see as far as Cannock Chase, the Wrekin, the Welsh mountains and even Merseyside.

Doxey Pool is rumoured to be named after the beautiful daughter of Bess Bower. She was carried off one day by strange men and thereafter her mother languished, and died of grief.

Kinver and the Million

Start The car park beneath Holy Austin Rock, DY7 6DL, GR 836836

Distance 7 miles (11.2km)

Summary Easy

Maps OS Landranger 138 and 139

Where to eat and drink There is a selection of pubs and facilities in Kinver

A fine walk near Kinver.

1️⃣ From the car park, walk down to the end of Meddin's Lane; at Potter's Cross by the T-junction turn left, then right along Hyde Lane as far as the last house on the right. Take the signed bridlepath to the right to the Hyde, as far as the hexagonal building.

2️⃣ There you find a bridleway to Dunsley, and a bridge over the river. In a few yards, and before the bridge, take the footpath on the left. Follow this through the woodland to a hunter's gate into a pasture, and go up a slight rise and over a stile into a field. Cross to another stile and a road.

3️⃣ Turn right along the road to the Staffordshire and Worcestershire Canal. Turn left along the towpath, and continue as far as Prestwood Bridge.

4️⃣ Here, turn left along an unsurfaced road to reach a surfaced road, which you cross; then go up a sunken bridleway opposite to join a farm road. Go left on this road, passing Gothersley Farm and Hall to enter woodland and The Million. Follow the path for about a mile to a road. Cross and continue through woodland to emerge on to the A458. Go right along the road to a sharp right-hand bend in front of Enville Hall.

5️⃣ Turn left for a few yards to the entrance to the Hall on the right, and go up the drive to the Hall buildings. Turn left, and follow the road to Home Farm; where the road turns right, you go straight ahead along a sunken pathway to another road at an acute bend.

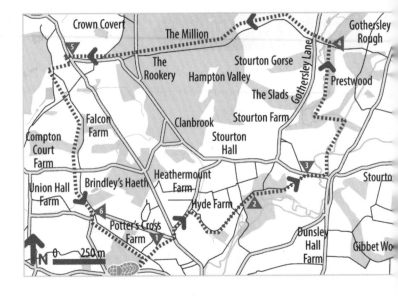

6 Turn right, and in approximately 100yd take the Staffordshire Way footpath on the left between stone posts. Follow this path along the edge of a field and through a pasture to a stile at the back of houses. Go through, and follow the path and road through the estate; finally turn right for the car park.

Points of interest

Enville Hall is the home of the Earls of Stamford, dating mostly from the eighteenth century.

Kinver Edge is known for its 'rock houses' carved out of the sandstone; the last occupants of these were rehoused as recently as 1950.

Onecote, Butterton and Mixon

START Off road at the village hall, Onecote, ST13 7RU, GR 049551

MAPS OS Landranger 119, Explorer OL24

DISTANCE 7 miles (11.2km)

SUMMARY Moderate

WHERE TO EAT AND DRINK The Jervis Arms in Onecote, T01538 304206

A walk on the moors around Onecote and Butterton.

[1] Go down to the main road and turn left; then turn right up a track 50yd beyond a farm drive. At the first bend, go left over a stile and follow the telegraph poles to cross a second stile. A clear path crosses the moor. At the road, go straight over and along the track towards Twist Green. At its end, continue by crossing the stile near the corner of the facing wall. The way ahead is via stiles on a clear path across several very narrow fields. Go right partway down the last field, and over a stile on to a walled path, followed by steps descending to the ford in Butterton.

[2] Turn left and walk up the road through the village, keeping left at all junctions until you reach Dog Lane where you turn right. At the top of the rise, cross the stile on the left, go diagonally right through two fields, and follow the hedge through the next two fields to a road. Cross the waymarked stile opposite as directed, crossing a stream, and go through a wooden gate. Keep left of a stone building on to a track. Go over a waymarked stile on the right. Continue as directed, along a hollow-way, across a stream, up the slope opposite and down a grassy hollow-way. Go up the hillside, cross a stile on the right, and keep ahead across the hillside to a farm drive and waymarker. Go left through a gate into the yard, then right as signed, through a gate to a stile. Continue as signed, crossing a footbridge and stile off to the right before following the path round the farm to a footpath junction. Cross the stile, and the one opposite, and follow the boundary fence over a stile and footbridge.

3 At the far end of the field, turn left by the wall and ascend to Under the Hill Farm. Turn left through the farm. Go through a gate and over a stile, then obliquely right to pick up a boundary hedge. Partway along cross a stile, then turn left along the hedge to cross two more stiles into Breech Farm yard. Go right and right again on the access road to a gate and waymarked stile. Yellow arrows mark the way ahead to and through the yard of Blackbrook Farm.

4 Follow the footpath sign for Mixon along a rough track for a short distance, then go left over a waymarked stile. Continue to follow waymarks through to the site of the old Mixon copper mine. Take the footpath signed for Mowidge to a rough track; here turn left and follow the trail. Beyond Onecote Grange you reach the roadway where you turn left, then left again at the crossroads, back to the start point.

The Canal near Wombourne

START The Bratch car park, WV5 8DH, GR 868937

DISTANCE 7 miles (11.2km)

SUMMARY Easy

MAPS OS Landranger 139

WHERE TO EAT AND DRINK There are various pubs and services in Wombourne

A walk through semi-rural areas to the south of Wolverhampton.

[1] Leave the Bratch car park and join the Staffordshire and Worcestershire Canal towpath. Head north past the locks and the unusual octagonal toll office as far as Bridge 52, where the towpath changes banks. Continue to follow the towpath reaching the feeder reservoirs and arrive at Mops Farm bridge (Bridge 54).

[2] Cross over the bridge and follow a track that brings you to Castle Croft Lane. Cross the lane and walk along Castlecroft Road, past the hotel as far as Bhylls Lane.

[3] Turn right on to the Kingswinford railway walk. A very pleasant stroll eventually brings you back to Wombourne and the Bratch car park.

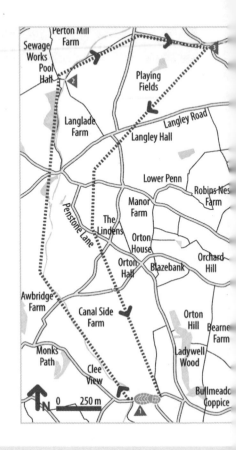

Points of interest

The Staffordshire and Worcestershire canal was built by James Brindley and opened in 1772 to connect the Trent and Mersey rivers with the Severn. From the outset it was a success, being well placed to bring goods from the Potteries and Birmingham to Bristol and the West Country.

Kingswinford railway was completed in 1925, however it made substantial losses on its passenger traffic and fell victim to Dr Beeching's 'axe' and was closed. In 1981 the county council opened it as a walk.

Okeover and Ilam

START On the roadside above
Okeover Bridge near Mapleton, or in
the village, DE6 2AB, GR 165482

DISTANCE 7 miles (11.2km)

SUMMARY Moderate

MAPS OS Landranger 119

WHERE TO EAT AND DRINK The
Okeover Arms in Mapleton, http://
theokeover.co.uk, T01335 350305;
food is served Mon–Fri 12.00–
3.00pm and 6.00–9.00pm, Sat and
Sun 12.00–9.00pm

A steady ascent through Okeover Park and an easy walk to Ilam, with fine views towards Dovedale.

[1] Cross the bridge, and on the left is a ladder stile. Cross this and veer left to cross a road; follow the footpath just to the left of a group of trees. Follow this uphill and through a timber gate towards a derelict house. Go straight ahead to the gap in the wood, cross the stile, go along the wood edge, and aim straight across the field going slightly right to a gate with a footpath signpost. Go through this, and swerve round an enclosure in the middle of the next field to a stile that leads on to a track leading to a farm.

[2] Go through the gate at the end of the track, and turn right. Go through another gate, on the right of the farm, and then over another stile to reach a path along the left field boundary. Follow the path across three fields to join a walled track to Woodhouses Farm. Go through the gate, and pass the farm buildings; when you reach a narrow lane that leads to Blore, turn right up it. Continue over the crossroads to Blore Pastures picnic site.

[3] Walk through the picnic area, cross the stile at the far end, and angle down the field to cross a second stile; the route rejoins the road near the bottom of the hill. Continue along the road to the bridge over the river at the entrance to Ilam village. The village is worth a visit.

[4] Cross the stile at the bridge right corner, and follow the clear path along the river, past its confluence with the River Dove. Now take a

waymarked path across the fields to Coldwall Bridge.

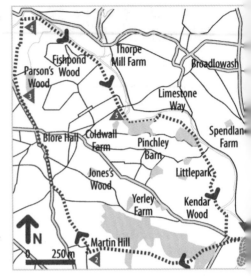

⑤ Go straight over the approach track, but not over the bridge, then through a stile in the wall, and follow this path to a track along the right bank of the river. Follow this through a small wood and along a clear path, which swings away from the river and into another small wood. As you enter, take a footpath waymarked to the right and up to a stile. Go over this, and proceed in a similar direction to reach a track adjacent to a farm. Turn right along the track for 100yd, then go left to cross a stile. Head across the large field to a stile in the left corner just down from a copse. Cross the next field in a similar fashion, to arrive at the river again; from here the path goes straight across the field to an old mill building and the road. Turn left along the road to regain the start.

Points of interest

Ilam is an estate village mostly demolished prior to alpine-style cottages being built. The Hall was built in the 1820s and partly demolished in the 1930s. The National Trust now owns it, and part is run as a youth hostel. The church has a Saxon blocked door and wall, and a Saxon or Norman font. The tower base is thirteenth century. The South Chapel contains a shrine to St Bertram with a ninth-century tomb cover.

Paradise Walk is a delightful scenic riverside path.

Coldwall Bridge was built in 1726; it carried the Cheadle to Thorpe turnpike road.

Okeover Park

START The layby on the A52, DE6 2HR, GR 145470

DISTANCE 7½ miles (12km)

SUMMARY Easy

MAPS OS Landranger 119

WHERE TO EAT AND DRINK The Dog & Partridge at Swinscoe (1 mile up the A52 road), www.dogandpartridge. co.uk, T01335 343183

A circular walk round Okeover Park.

[1] Cross the road and go slightly right to cross a stile, then go diagonally left across the field to a stile in the left boundary. Cross this to follow the footpath across more fields and stiles, and crossing the drive to Lower Grounds Farm. Pass to the left of the farm and continue in a similar direction to join the track to Martin Hill Farm. Go through another gate, on the right of the farm, and then over another stile to reach a path along the left field boundary. Follow the path across three fields to join a walled track to Woodhouses Farm. Go through the gate, pass the farm buildings, and reach a narrow lane that leads to Blore. Continue to a crossroads.

[2] Here turn right following the road, which is an old eighteenth-century turnpike road, to Coldwall Farm. Turn left down the farm drive to a rough track beyond, and enter a field via a gate. A footpath descends steeply in a direct line to Coldwall Bridge.

[3] Turn right through a stile in the right wall on the approach to the bridge, and follow this path to a track along the right bank of the river. Follow this through a small wood and along a clear path, which swings away from the river and into another small wood. As you enter, take a footpath waymarked to the right, which leads up to a stile. Go over this and proceed in a similar direction to reach a track adjacent to a farm. Turn right along the track for 100yd, then go left to cross a stile. Head across the large field to a stile in the left corner just down from a copse. Cross the next field to arrive at the river again; from here, the path goes straight across the field to an old mill building and the road.

④ Continue straight ahead on the road to enter Okeover Park, and then veer right, off the road, and follow a footpath just to the left of a group of trees. Follow this uphill and through a timber gate towards a derelict house. Go straight ahead to the gap in the wood, cross the stile, go along the wood edge, and then aim straight across the field bearing slightly right to a gate with a footpath signpost. Go through this, swerve round an enclosure in the middle of the next field, and continue to a stile on to a track leading to a farm.

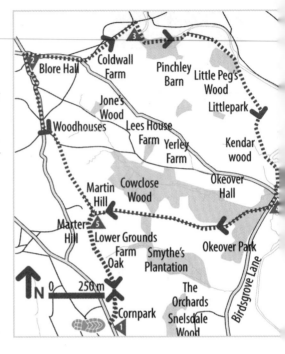

⑤ Go through the gate at the end of the track, and turn left. Retrace the outward section to regain the main road and the layby where you started.

Points of interest

Blore has a small fourteenth-century church and a sixteenth-century hall.

Okeover Hall and Park are privately owned, the family seat of the Okeover family, who have been in residence since Norman times.

Hollinsclough and the Moors

START From the car parking on the side of the road near the phone box at Hollinsclough, SK17 0RH, GR 065665

DISTANCE 7 miles (11.2km)

SUMMARY Moderate

MAPS OS Landranger 119, Explorer OL24

WHERE TO EAT AND DRINK Nothing on route

A walk for those who like quiet ways; there are impressive views throughout.

[1] Take the road uphill past the chapel, and turn right through a gate on to a path. At its end, turn on to a wide grassy path up the hillside. At a wall corner turn left, and go through two gates into Moorside Farm, leaving along the drive to a road. Turn right, then take a stile on the left, and cross the field down to a stile and brook beyond. Cross these and another stile ahead.

[2] Then go up to the top of the field, and left through a gate, then left through another into Wilshaw Farm yard. Bear slightly right to go through a gate/stile, and then follow a wide path up the hillside. Keep above a steep escarpment, and follow the waymarked path round to the right of Hill Top Farm, to cross its drive over stiles. In the next field go right to a wall stile and the road. Cross to the stile opposite. Go left down a track, and at a signpost, descend right to a stile. Cross and go downhill to cross two footbridges. Angle left up the slope and over a stile to follow a path that veers to the right of Hole Carr Farm, and so to its drive: follow this as it climbs steadily up to a road.

[3] Turn left along the road, go a little way, then turn right along the drive to Hocker Farm. Go over a stile on the left. Follow the top fence a short way before turning left to cross the field to a stile in the opposite corner. Go over the next field to a stile in the wall near a brook. Follow a similar direction to reach a stile/gate adjacent to

Oakenclough Hall. Take the track straight ahead, and where it ends in a field, turn right to a walled track between houses to go out to a road. Go left to a road junction, and continue for just a few more yards.

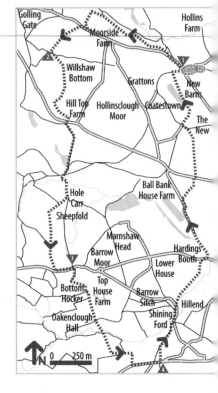

④ Then take a stile on the left on to a permissive path, which takes you through a field and over another stile on the left. In the next field go down to the right and follow a waymarked path to cross a stile in the left wall, across another field and stile to join the lane at Shining Ford. Turn left, and shortly turn right over a stile. Follow the wall to a stile on the left, and continue round a farm to join the lane. Go right, then turn left to follow a lane; shortly after a small S bend, cross the stile on the right. Cross fields up to a stile in the top wall on to Fawside Edge Farm drive and the road. Go over the stile opposite. Follow the boundary wall over three more stiles to reach a narrow lane. Turn left, then right at the junction, and descend along a stone-walled track to Hollinsclough and the start.

Points of interest

The chapel (Bethel) in Hollinsclough was built in 1801 by John Lomas, a jaggerman (leader of packhorse trains).

Hollinsclough was once known for its silk-spinning cottage industry. It is set in the shadow of Chrome (pronounced 'Kroom') Hill, a limestone reef known locally as the 'Dragon's Back'.

Bradley and Coppenhall ▶

START The Webb Stone in Bradley, ST18 9DW, GR 880180

DISTANCE 7½ miles (12km)

SUMMARY Easy

MAPS OS Landranger 127

WHERE TO EAT AND DRINK The Red Lion, Bradley, www.redlionbradley.co.uk, T01785 780297; The Bell, Haughton, www.the bellhoughton.co.uk, T01785 780301

A straightforward walk from Bradley, a handsome Staffordshire village.

[1] Leaving the stone, make your way to the 500-year-old church, and turn right along the road at its side. With a school behind you, walk to the end of the road and a junction. Ahead is a waymark stile. Go over this, and over another double stile into a sloping field. Head towards the gate in the bottom left corner. Go through it, and follow a hedged and gated green lane for a short distance to another gate. Go to the far left corner of the field and cross over a stile. Follow the left hedge in the next field to a farm track: ahead is a waymarker, then a gate. Go through the gate, passing barns on the right. Go through another gate, keeping to the right edge of the field up the hill as far as the double reservoir gates at the top. In the corner the route appears to be blocked by wire, but go along the wire fence for a few yards and there is a section where the top strand of wire can be unhooked to allow you to cross. Continue to the remains of a windmill.

[2] Here, go down the hedge track and through the yard at Butterhill Farm. Go left, and left again to join a tarmac lane. Go right to a T-junction, and turn left, then right, to a lane into Coppenhall. At the next junction go left, for Stafford, to the end of the village, and then right along Chase View Lane. At the second sharp left-hand bend, by a farm, take the gate on the right, and then a second gate immediately on the left. Follow

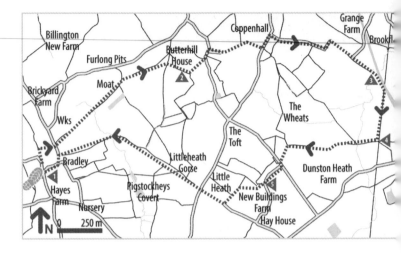

the left hedge through another gate and continue on the same line towards a low sandy embankment. Although there may be a barbed wire fence here, it can be unfastened to allow you to cross. Continue until you reach a stream.

③ The stream runs through a culvert under the motorway, but just before this there is a crossing point: cross here as best you can, and go right, along the motorway edge to the railway. Turn right and continue as far as the next railway bridge.

④ Turn right here away from the bridge along a path that crosses a stream. Bear slightly right away from the telegraph poles to an inverted corner and a ditch. The path is now a straight line all the way to Valley Farm, but unfortunately it is not stiled until you reach one on to the farm drive. Go left to a road and turn left, then immediately right: this will bring you to a cottage and a bend in the lane with a footpath sign on the right.

⑤ Go through the gate and over the stile opposite, bearing right through a gate by a water trough. Go half left to a field corner, passing a pool, and going through a hunter's gate. Go through the gate to join a track, from a stile, to the road.

At the road go right to a road junction, and there follow the no-through-road. The made road soon becomes a distinct bridleway, passing several pools to a gateway into a field. Go forward with the hedge on your right, and at the end of the field go through the wide gap. Go half left over a footbridge and stile. Follow the right hedge to a hunter's gate into a sunken lane, which climbs back up to the Webb Stone.

Points of interest

The Webb Stone: legend has it that to avoid spinsterhood, local maidens should bow to the stone whenever they pass it. It is one of three standing stones in Bradley. According to the legend, the stones were stolen from the church by the devil so that he could use them to build hell, but he dropped them on his way home! The Webb Stone is also said to spin round and has an additional local name of 'The Wanderer'.

START The small car park behind the parish hall opposite the church, DE6 2HB, GR 116435

DISTANCE 7½ miles (12km)

SUMMARY Moderate, with a steep section up to the summit

MAPS OS Landranger 128

WHERE TO EAT AND DRINK The Duncombe Arms in Ellastone, www.duncombearms.co.uk/, T01335 324275, Mon–Thurs 12–2.30pm and 6–9pm, Fri and Sat 12–2.30pm and 5.30–10pm, Sun 12–8pm

A walk from the George Elliot village of Upper Ellaston to the summit of the Weaver Hills.

1 Turn left up Church Lane. After 300yd, go right at a footpath sign into a field. Go left of the farm down to a stile; the route then follows yellow arrow waymarkers across stiles and footbridges uphill to reach a gate in an iron fence at Wootton Hall Farm. Go through and across the paddock to a stile on the right of the farm, and on to a track. Turn right and join Hall Lane. Turn left and go along Hall Lane into Wootton. Go through the village and on to the Leek road; just after Show Croft Farm, turn right on a rough track (Gidacre Lane).

2 Where the track ends, and a gate leads into the cricket ground on the left, cross the wooden stile in the corner of the hedge, and cross the field to the diagonally opposite corner where there are double wooden gates. Go through, and cross the next field to the far left wall and into the next field. Head up to the diagonally opposite corner and over a stile. Continue left and around the hillside to a stile, after which the route levels out and continues around a wall corner; cross more stiles that are clearly marked as leading to the summit of the hill over on the left. The views from the summit are extensive. Retrace your steps from here back into the field, and follow the right edge to a stile.

3 Go through to a reasonably clear path and along the left field boundary. Proceed in this similar direction across fields to an unfenced lane. Turn right, and shortly cross a cattle grid.

4 Turn right on to open land. Follow the fence and wall on the right (ignore the stile you pass), and go to the bottom right corner to a stile and squeezer stile, and cross into a field. Go across the field to the hedge opposite, and cross a stone stile. Follow the hedge on the left to the bottom left corner and a low stone wall. Cross into a field, and go across it to a gate; go through into another field and cross this field also, to a stile in a hedge. Cross into a garden, and go out through a gate. Cross the drive to a squeezer stile in a stone wall. Go diagonally left to a stile in the hedge, and cross on to Back Lane in Wootton.

5 Turn right along the road to a T-junction with Hall Lane. Turn left, and return to Upper Ellastone along the outward route.

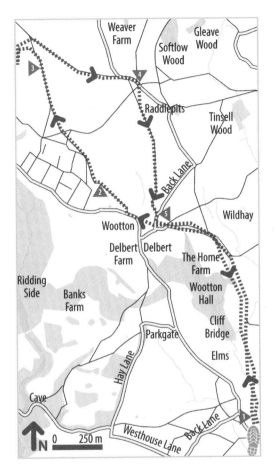

83 Longnor and Reaps Moor

START The car park in Longnor Market, SK17 0NT, GR 088649

DISTANCE 7½ miles (12km)

SUMMARY Fairly easy

MAPS OS Landranger 119

WHERE TO EAT AND DRINK Ye Old Cheshire Cheese in Longnor, www.cheshirecheeselongnor.co.uk, T01298 83218. Also The Pack Horse Inn in Crowdecote, www.thepackhorseinn.co.uk, T01298 83618, Wed–Sun food served until 2.30pm, and 9pm. Also in Longnor, Cobbles Café, www.cobblescafe.co.uk, T01298 83166 Thurs–Sun 8.30am–4pm (ish)

A walk through river meadows and over moorland with superb views throughout.

1 Turn left from the car park along the road past the Cheshire Cheese Inn. Take the footpath on the right into a farmyard, turning left in the middle to cross a stile in the corner. Go diagonally right across a field, and follow the clearly stiled path along the banks of the River Manifold, passing Lower Boothlow Farm. Continue in a similar line to reach a barn by Ridge End Farm.

2 At this point the route turns right to cross a stile by a gate. Go straight ahead through the right-hand gate, and diagonally across to a footbridge. Beyond this, turn left along a track and go over a corner stile. Go along the left field edge, over a wooden stile near the corner, and 60yd on, turn left over a second wooden stile. Go diagonally right to a road and turn left. Turn right at the junction, and opposite a farm go left to cross a footbridge. Head right, cross a stile, and follow the right boundary to the road.

3 Cross, and continue up the hillside to a stile in the wall in the top left corner. Go over this, and veer right to another stile in the right-hand wall. Continue along the wall past a derelict cottage and over two more stiles. Follow the left-hand wall to another road.

4 Cross, and go over two stiles, then around left to cross a third stile. Follow the wall to a gate near a barn.

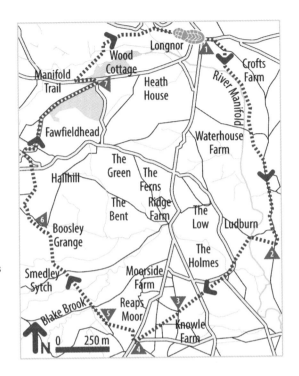

5 Go through this, and along the left boundary. Go over two stiles and a footbridge to a stile left of a gate. Go over, keep along the left boundary, and head in a similar direction across stiles and fields to a stile/gate in the corner. From here, follow the hedge on the left to a track by Boosley Grange. Turn left, through a gate and along a wide path.

6 Just beyond the end of the right boundary fence, turn right to cross a stream to a stile on the left in the field corner. Climb the field beyond to a stile/gate on to a track passing Bank House up to a road. Cross this to another track, and reach a narrow lane. Go left, then right, and on to the lane. Pass Lane Farm, and through a gate to a deep hollow way. Continue on a lane to a T-junction.

7 Turn left, and left again. At the end of the trees turn right over a stile and drop down to a footbridge over the River Manifold. Now head for a farm. Go through the yard and then along the drive for a few yards until you see a clear field path on the right. Take this across three fields, then turn diagonally right to pass through a stile in the wall corner. Follow the path to a farm access road, and go straight on to Longnor.

84 Wall and Packington Moor

START The Roman site of Wall off the A5, WS14 0AW, GR 096065

DISTANCE 8 miles (13km)

SUMMARY Easy

MAPS OS Landranger 139

WHERE TO EAT AND DRINK The Trooper Inn in Wall, www.thetrooperwall. co.uk, T01543 480413

1 From the site entrance walk up the main street as far as the Trooper Inn, and turn left to follow the road to a signpost for Lichfield. Turn right, and follow the lane to a junction with a road. Turn right again to another road junction. Opposite is a clear track across the fields, which runs under a railway bridge and comes out at a road. Turn left along the road to a junction with the A5127. Opposite are double gates: go through these, and follow a track for ½ mile to the far corner of a huge field. Go over the fence to your right, and down the busy A5148 with the fence on the left. At the road fence go through the gate on the left to cross over the road bridge; you will come to a pool in front of houses. Turn left to join a surfaced lane.

2 Here, turn left to the dual carriageway A38. Cross it, and take the drive ahead, which soon becomes a wide track; continue for almost a mile to, and through, the gates at Freeford Home Farm.

3 Turn right between the house and farm, and keep going until you come to a surfaced lane. Cross this, and take the green lane opposite. Pass a small stand of trees on the right, and you will soon arrive at a gate and a line of trees where there is a junction of tracks.

4 Turn right and continue to a minor road, which you cross: take the green track opposite, and shortly you will reach the A38. Cross the road using the central reservation, and turn right. At the sign for Swinfen Hall take the bridleway left, and a little over ½ mile later you come to another minor road. Cross this and go through the gate opposite, and follow the left-hand hedge and

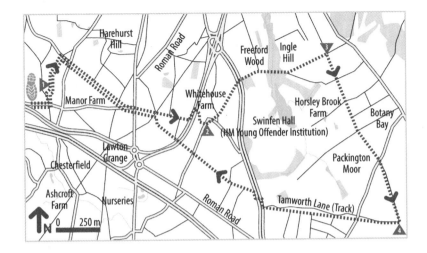

fence to a stile to the A5148. Cross the road and the stile opposite and continue to follow the left-hand hedge and fence. Change to the right side near the overhead power lines to go through a gate and rejoin the track that you walked earlier. From here, retrace your steps all the way back to the T-junction with the sign for Lichfield, and here turn right to the village church. Turn left along the church wall to reach The Butts, and so return to the Wall site.

Points of interest

Wall: strategically placed on Watling Street, this Romano-British settlement was a military establishment that protected Watling Street and nearby Ryknild Street. The settlement also served as a resting place for official and civilian wayfarers travelling in either direction, and as a result, a significant service town grew up around the garrison.

Alstonfield and Damgate

START The public car park at
Milldale, DE6 2AY, GR 135548

DISTANCE 8 miles (13km)

SUMMARY Moderate

MAPS OS Landranger 119, Explorer
OL24

WHERE TO EAT AND DRINK The
George at Alstonefield, www.
thegeorgeatalstonefield.com,
T01335 310 205, Mon–Thurs
11.30am–3pm and 6–11pm, Fri and
Sat 11.30am–11pm, Sun 12–9.30pm

A high-level walk with excellent views.

1 Go down the road into Milldale, and take a lane on the left between
two cottages. Follow the lane, which climbs up to Alstonefield past the
church and manor house, before turning left alongside the village green.
Continue to the road ahead.

2 Go straight across on a rough track to a stile adjacent to a stone
barn. Cross the field ahead to a stile near the left corner, beyond which a
clear path crosses two fields to a narrow lane. Cross the lane and the stile
opposite, and continue on another well trodden path, keeping ahead at
footpath crossroads to reach a second lane via a paddock, footbridge and
stiles. Across the lane the route continues up the field just right of a large
tree. Go through a corner stile to follow the wall left for a short distance,
before cutting off the field corner to join the Wetton road at a footpath
sign. Turn right to the T-junction, then right again on to Wetton main
street. Take the first turn left, and pass the public toilets and car park.

3 You will reach an old barn on the left with an adjacent wall stile. Cross
this and climb up the field, heading for the large tree at the top and the
wall stile just beyond it. Go over and follow the field boundary to cross the
lane at the bottom via two stiles. Looking ahead, a clear narrow path can
be seen, which goes up and along the hillside, giving superb views over
part of the Manifold Valley and the moors beyond. Follow the path past
the remains of lead mines to a National Trust sign. Turn left to cross a wall
stile on to a clear path through the remains of the Highfields mine.

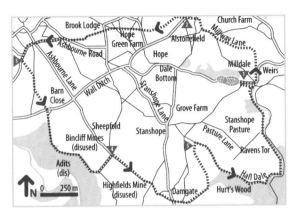

④ At the footpath crossroads with a tall footpath sign, turn right and follow the left boundary straight through to Damgate Farm. Keep ahead past the farm and through a gate, then go left, immediately over a stile to reach another in the far right corner. Go over on to a road. Opposite, and a little right, go over a stile and cross a field and a stile in far right corner on to a walled track. Go left, and after 200yd, left again past a wood end to continue along the left boundary.

⑤ Descend to cross a stile into Hall Dale. Walk down the dale to meet the River Dove before turning left for an attractive walk along the river. The path leaves the river for a while, continuing clearly across fields and through a wood. At the road turn left, and walk down the short, steep descent to Milldale.

Points of interest

Wetton: the village has Saxon origins. The church has a fourteenth-century tower, though the remainder is nineteenth century. Some of the village houses date from the sixteenth and seventeenth centuries.

Milldale: the packhorse bridge, known as Viator's Bridge, is referred to in the 1676 edition of Izaak Walton's *Compleat Angler*.

Alstonefield was originally a Saxon settlement, and once a busy market town – its charter was granted in 1308 – and the crossroads of several packhorse ways. The church is the third on the same site and has a Norman south doorway, chancel arch and fine seventeenth-century pews.

86 Around Blackwell

START Miller's Dale old station pay and display car park, SK17 8SN, GR 138732

DISTANCE 8½ miles (14km)

SUMMARY Can be strenuous in parts over bare rocks and up steep hillsides; otherwise the route is fairly level

MAPS OS Landranger 119

WHERE TO EAT AND DRINK The Angler's Rest in Miller's Dale, www.theanglersrest.co.uk, T01298 871323; food is served daily 12.30–14.30 and 18.30–20.30

A varied walk on lanes, field paths and riverside paths.

Walk away from the car park entrance to the end of the old platforms and take a path, left, down to the River Wye where you come to the road. Go right over the bridge and up the road for 25yd to the speed sign, and take a footpath across on the left. Shortly you come to a footpath sign and a stepped path up the hillside on the right. This is the shortest way to the top. There is a slightly easier way, where you go straight on to a gate and through the gap at the side, and turn right up a flight of steps; at the top of the steps turn right on to a path which brings you to where it joins the other steep footpath. Continue up the stepped path to the top, and cross a stile into a field. Cross the field to a stile in the top left-hand corner by a gate and a tree. Take the same line across two more fields – the stiles are obvious – to reach a bend in a track. Go right and follow it to a lane.

① Turn left up the lane for ½ mile to a road, and keep ahead for a few yards to a crossroads. Turn right to the main A6. Cross the road, and go up the track on the left of the Waterloo Hotel. After about ½ mile go round a hairpin bend.

② Just beyond the bend go over a signposted stile on the right; the path heads left, and in the second field Fivewells Farm comes into view. The footpath goes through the farm to pick up the farm drive.

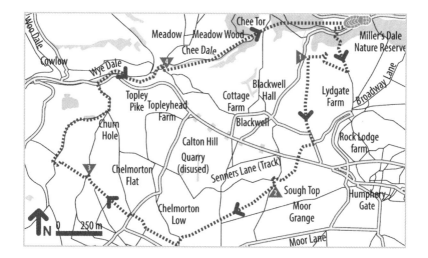

At the end of the drive cross the lane and go through the pedestrian gate to follow the footpath to Chelmorton. Then go down the road between the church and Church Inn to a junction: turn right here along a signposted track, passing Shepley Farm, as far as a road. Go left, then right on to another track for ¾ mile to a junction of tracks, and turn left.

③ After a few yards go over a stile on the right, and head across the field to another stile built into the drystone wall. Cross two more fields in similar fashion to the edge of Deep Dale. The path zig-zags steeply down beside a cave to the dale bottom. In the dale go right for about a mile: it's a bit rough over rocky sections, and marred by a working quarry at the end where you come to the main road A6. Cross the road and take the track right through the car park until you come to a footbridge over the river.

④ Here, follow signs to the right up on to the Monsall Trail for an easy, level walk along the old railway and through tunnels back to the start.

START **The Commonwealth cemetery,** WS12 4PS, GR 983154

DISTANCE **9 miles (14.5km)**

SUMMARY **Easy**

MAPS **OS Landranger 127, 128**

WHERE TO EAT AND DRINK **Nothing on route**

A thought-provoking walk.

1 From the cemetery, continue along the service road to the entrance of the German cemetery. Opposite are some steps: climb these to reach, and follow, a path through woodland to a road. Cross over and follow the same line on a path through trees to a second road. Go through the car park opposite, and passing over a vehicle barrier, continue for a few yards to a junction of tracks. Here take the track to the right of a signed blue route, and gradually drop down Brindley Valley to a small car park and road.

2 Go left along the road for 80yd, and turn right along the road signed for the picnic area. At the top, bear right and then go left through a barrier; follow the grass-covered tarmac path up to the T-junction with the perimeter tarmac. Cross the perimeter, bearing very slightly left, to a gap in the trees and Marquis Drive. For the last half mile you have been crossing the former RAF training camp. Turn left along Marquis Drive for a short distance, then go right down a track, following the power line, to the valley bottom and a pool on your left. At the track junction go right; you will pass the nature reserve sign, and then a series of pools, and will come to a track T-junction.

3 Go right and cross Stony Brook by a footbridge over the ford, and continue along the wide forestry road to reach terraced houses and a road. Turn right along the road to its junction with the A460; go across and right, down a service road, and then left into Mifflin's Valley. Walk through the valley, and at the top of a slight rise take the lesser track on the right; you will soon meet a major cross track.

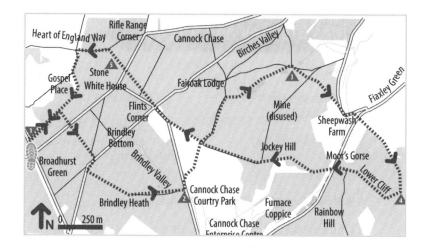

(4) Turn right, and in a short distance you will see a small pool on the left of a right bend: this is the whimsically named Seven Springs. Continuing along the track, cross the A460 and the level crossing, and ascend Marquis Drive, which progresses from path to track to tarmac over its 1½-mile length, till a road is reached. Go right to a finger post and cross to the Birches Valley road sign. Slightly right of this sign is a footpath between trees: follow it – over two cross tracks – to a road called Penkridge Bank. Go through the vehicle barrier opposite, and follow the edge of the heathland and forestry down to a track junction.

(5) Turn left to the Sherbrooke Valley, and then left again back to the car park.

Points of interest

During the 1914–18 war, Cannock Chase was one vast British and Commonwealth training camp. During this period a major epidemic decimated the trainees, and the first cemetery at the start of this walk contains the graves of many of the victims. The second cemetery – the German cemetery – contains the graves of participants from both conflicts.

Kings Bromley and Alrewas

Start A side street off the A515, DE13 7HE, GR 128175

Distance 9 miles (14.5km)

Summary Easy

Maps OS Landranger 128

Where to eat and drink The Crown in Alrewas, www.crownalrewas.co.uk , T 01283 791217

A level walk through the Trent Valley water meadows.

[1] Turn left along the A515, keeping safely to verges and the layby along the main road until you reach Yoxall Bridge. Cross the fence just before it on the right, and follow the River Trent downstream over two stiles. Where the river goes into a left bend, take a stile at the side of a double gate, and follow the green lane to two gates on the left.

[2] Go through the second gate, and follow the hedge on the left to a gateway in the field corner. Now follow the right-hand hedge/fence to a protruding corner, and from there go across the field to meet the river bank and a stiled foot bridge. Go over three stiles along the riverside, the last one taking you on a slight diversion: over the stile you leave the river and follow the hedge on the right, keeping with it as it veers slightly right, to reach another protruding corner where you go straight across the field to a stile in the corner – to the left can be seen Wychnor Hall and park. Continue with the hedge on your left to cross a ditch. Go half right to a gate and stile. Turn right along the green lane for a few yards to a gate on the left, with a plank bridge and stile almost next to it. Cross the stile and go slightly right, through a break in the hedge, to a gateway; go through this, and on to a second, which is in line with Alrewas church tower. Follow a barely distinguishable track half right over a ditch and through a gate. Swing left with the ditch to another gate, where you almost meet the river again. In the next field go half right to the far corner. Turn left along the fence path to a cul-de-sac.

[3] Turn right to the junction with Church Road, then left to pass the church, continuing through Alrewas to the canal bridge. At the canal

bridge turn right along the towpath, and follow it for almost 2 miles to the road at Keepers Lock. Turn right along the road; shortly after on a right bend go left between the houses, and along the concrete farm road to reach Alrewas Hays. Follow the drive to the left of the house.

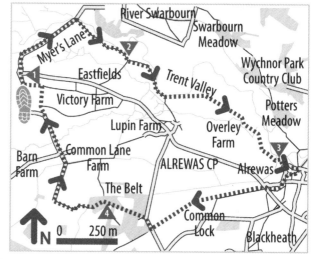

④ Then go straight over a grassed area with woods on your left; you will reach a track where you go left, with the woods still on your left, and will soon come to a junction of tracks. Go right down to a sleeper bridge over a brook. Cross the brook and continue straight ahead across and up the field to a hedge. Go left with the hedge to the entrance of a green lane on the right. Follow this very pleasant lane forwards and right to join a tarmac lane. Continue forwards again to a left bend in the lane at Woodgate. Directly ahead is a stile, which you cross, and two more stiles heading towards a pylon; there go half left to a stile in a playing field. Now go diagonally right to the right corner of the field, where you come out on to the road. Turn right to the A515, and the side road where you started is on the left.

Points of interest

Alrewas is a restful place with some interesting timbered and thatched buildings. On the edge of the village, the River Trent actually joins the Trent and Mersey Canal.

89

90

Froghall and Consall

START The Froghall picnic area, ST10 2HJ, GR 027476

DISTANCE 9 miles (14.5km) or 11 miles (17.5km)

SUMMARY Easy

MAPS OS Landranger 119

WHERE TO EAT AND DRINK The Black Lion at Consall Forge, www.blacklionpub.co.uk, T01782 550294, Mon–Sat 12 noon–11pm, Sun 12 noon–10.30pm

An easy and interesting walk along the Caldon Canal. The longer option goes to the Consall Nature Park.

1 From Froghall picnic area take the road to a path that follows the left side of the canal. Continue along the path. When the canal disappears into a tunnel under the Ipstone road, cross the road to pick up the path on the left of the canal again. Continue along the path; the view widens to include the River Churnet down to the left and wooded banks on either side. After approximately 1 mile you reach Cherryeye Bridge. Continue along the canal to a steel girder bridge, and cross over it to the other side. You will pass an old flint mill across the canal, then a canal lock. Eventually the canal runs very close to the railway line and a station. A little further on, the valley widens out, and the canal and river join at Consall Forge where there is a small pub, the Black Lion.

2 If you want to go on to the Consall Nature Park, cross the bridges over the canal and river, and turn left along the track. Where it joins a wide track turn right, uphill, and continue almost to the top; here a tarmac drive leads down to the Nature Park Centre. There is a choice of walks waymarked from here, and leaflets can be obtained in the centre. To return to Froghall, go back along the same route.

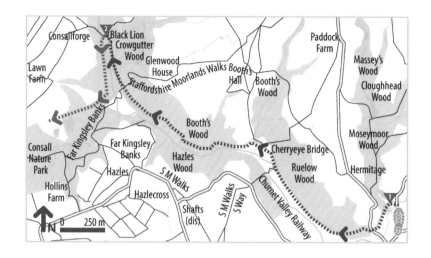

Points of interest

Cherryeye Bridge is said to have been given its name because the eyes of local miners were reddened by iron ore dust.
Consall Nature Park was opened in 1990.

Wheaton Aston and Mitton

START Hartley Arms, Wheaton Aston, ST19 9NF, GR 852126

DISTANCE 9 miles (14.5km)

SUMMARY Easy

MAPS OS Landranger 127

WHERE TO EAT AND DRINK The Hartley Arms, www.hartleyarms.co.uk, T01785 840232

A fine country walk, where kingfisher and heron sightings are common on the canal.

[1] From the Hartley Arms cross the Tavern bridge, and turn right to walk south-east along the Shropshire Union canal towpath. At the second bridge along the canal go left through a farm, and follow the Staffordshire way signs into Lapley. Turn left along a road, and turn right into the churchyard; go to the right of the church.

[2] As you enter the trees, turn left and go over a stile. After a few paces bear left and follow a path along a bank to a hunter's gate. Go through, and continue forwards to the corner of a stand of trees. Carry on to the end of the next field, and go left following a Staffordshire way sign to double hunter's gates on the right. Go through them into another field. Go diagonally left to a sign, next to a stile and gate, on the right of a large oak tree. Do not go over the stile, but continue along the left-hand hedge, following the Staffordshire way sign, to the gate into a farm.

[3] Turn right, and you will come to a stile and hunter's gate on your left. Go over these, bearing right to a gap in the fence, and through trees to reach another stile and hunter's gate. Go through, and continue with the hedge on your left. In the corner of this field go through a hunter's gate to cross Bickford Meadows, which is an area of scientific interest. Cross partly by duckboards over the marshy parts of the wetlands, and cross two footbridges to reach the distinctive track into Mitton. From the road at Mitton go forward to cross a small bridge, then turn left along a quiet surfaced lane almost 1½ miles to Sherdicote Hall farm.

④ Just beyond the farm the lane turns sharp right, but you go left between the hedges of an unsurfaced green lane. Soon the lane ends at two adjacent gates: go through the left-hand one to follow the right-hand hedge to a second gate. Go through to reach a third. In the next field cross to the hunter's gate and footbridge over a brook. Continue across the next field with the hedge on your left, to a stile and a plank footbridge.

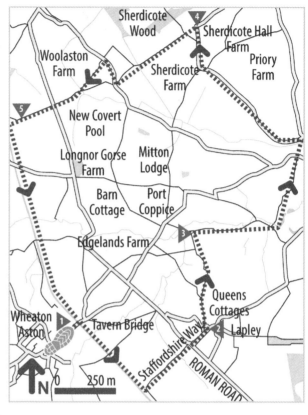

Cross these, and walk along the edge of the next field to the lane opposite a cottage. Turn right along the lane to as far as Lower Woolaston Farm; just beyond, a left turn along the hedged green lane will bring you to Rusty Pits. Go forward on the track with the hedge on your right to reach a lane. Cross over, and continue on a short green lane into a field. Walk with the hedge on your left to the final field before the trees.

⑤ Here, go half right to a gate on the edge of the trees. Through the gate is a path to a canal bridge. Go left along the towpath back to Wheaton Aston.

The Trent and Mersey Canal

START Along the side of the road at Keepers Lock near Fradley Junction, DE13 7DW, GR 144142

DISTANCE 6½ miles (10km)

SUMMARY Easy

MAPS OS Landranger 128

WHERE TO EAT AND DRINK There are various establishments around Fradley Junction

A fine, historical walk.

[1] Walk along the road with the canal on your left, passing Fradley Junction; cross the canal over the bridge at Shade House lock. Cross a stile on your right, and follow a path in a field on the left side of the canal; pick your way through scrub into woodland, still parallel with the canal on your right. After the woodland, follow a field edge to a road. Cross over the stile opposite, and follow the path over a field to a gateway/stile.

[2] Once through this, cross a tarmac strip/trackway, and look for a footbridge on the right in scrubland. Over the footbridge is a chain-link fence: go left and follow this fence for some distance. You will emerge from the scrub at a footbridge and stile into a field. Cross the field following the telegraph poles to the white house: you will arrive at the left corner of the garden fence. At this point aim for a gate in line with a pylon, and go on to a gravel track, which emerges at the road by a garden centre.

[3] Cross the road and go through the gate, where the line of your path is to the protruding field corner next to a pylon. At this point continue with the hedge on your right, and at the next corner go straight ahead and through a stile to follow the hedge. Aim for the stile over the railway line, but go along the edge of the field with the railway line on your left, ignoring the bridge across it, and veer off towards a hurdle stile. Follow the same line across several stiles and gates, until you meet the road to the right of a bungalow. Cross the road and go slightly left to pick up a track that you follow into

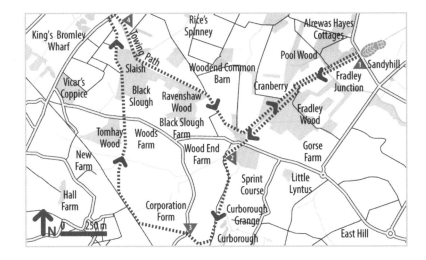

woodland. Where the track goes right, carry on along a grassy path at the woodland's edge, to a gate. Go through the gate, and straight on to meet the A515.

4 Go right to a canal bridge, and right again all along the canal towpath; eventually you will arrive back at Fradley Junction.

Alstonefield to Ecton Hill

START The public car park in
Alstonefield, DE6 2FY, GR 131556

DISTANCE 10 miles (16km)

SUMMARY Moderate

MAPS OS Landranger 119, Explorer
OL24

WHERE TO EAT AND DRINK The
George in Alstonefield, www.
thegeorgeatalstonefield.com,
T01335 310 205, Mon–Thurs
11.30am–3pm, 6pm–11pm, Fri and
Sat 11.30am–11pm, Sun 12pm–
9.30pm; food times vary

A fairly testing, mainly high-level walk with magnificent views.

1 Turn right from the car park, and right again at the junction,
then left at a T-junction, and immediately left again on to a track by a
house. Go over a stile. Follow the boundary wall and the well defined
path descending steeply to a road. Go right for about 300yd, and left
over a stile. Follow the path that turns sharply right up the slope to a
stile. Cross this, and the one over the road, and follow the wall up the
field. Go over two stiles before angling slightly left to pick up a clear
path ascending the field along a wall to arrive at a narrow track. Cross
straight over on a clear path to a wall stile.

2 Go over and turn right along a narrow path and reach a narrow lane.
Go over the stile opposite, and follow the wall to a stile at the top. Cross
this stile, and head to the far right corner.

3 Here turn right on the road into Wetton. Go left at the T-junction,
then leave the road at a sharp left turn to follow the track to Ecton.
At the end of the track go over the stile ahead and reach a clear path
descending the hill. Cross a small field over stiles, and you will get to
a small stream. Cross a second footbridge and stile on to a road, and
follow it to a fork, where you take the left branch. After 50yd turn right
through a gate and go along a well worn path past the ruins of a mine.
Go over a stile, then go slightly right to cross a stile by the wall corner.
Follow the wall and a wide grassy path to reach a stone building.

4 Turn left down a grassy path, then take the narrow path clearly seen ahead up the hillside and over the ridge to reach a line of trees. Turn left along the trees, go over a stile, and then follow the wall straight ahead to a gate. Go through and diagonally left through two fields, then turn left along the wall to reach the farm road. Turn right to a small spinney just beyond the fork.

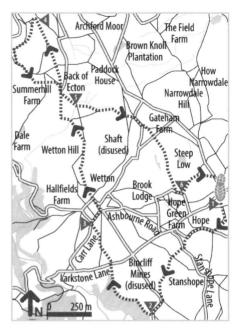

5 A clear path descends through the trees, and then goes diagonally across the following field. Continue straight ahead along the left side of the hill to arrive at a wall stile. Cross this and the field beyond to reach a road close to a tree plantation. Turn right for 100yd, then left on to a farm drive, immediately turning right across a field to a stile in the top left corner. Cross this, and two more ahead to reach another in the left wall just beyond Stoneham Barn. Go over, turn right, and keeping to the left of the boundary walls, cross a succession of stiles to reach a barn. The path then goes diagonally across two fields to reach a narrow lane.

6 Follow the lane for about 100yd to the left, then go left over a stile and follow the wall on a clear path, which swings right and ends at the road in Alstonefield. The car park is 200yd to the right.

Points of interest

Ecton Hill: there were some seventy lead and copper mines on the hill from the seventeenth to the nineteenth centuries. The stone building that you reach on the walk was once part of the engine house of the copper mine.

START On the roadside adjacent to the Roaches, ST13 8UA, GR 004621

DISTANCE 10 miles (16km)

SUMMARY Moderate with some challenging sections

MAPS OS Landranger 118 and 119

WHERE TO EAT AND DRINK Nothing on route

A gritstone ridge and moorlands walk with magnificent, wide-ranging views.

(1) Go through the small gate at the roadside, and turn right to follow the path to a stile in the right-hand wall. Take the path opposite which climbs the hillside, and continue along the foot of the Roaches. At the end of the rock face turn right up a clear path to reach the ridge summit. Continue on a steady ascent to a height and trig point with wide and extensive views over the Cheshire plain and Staffordshire moorlands. Descend to the narrow road at Roach End. Cross the road and stile opposite, and go straight ahead on a clear path for approximately 1 mile to reach a stile at a footpath crossroads.

(2) Go over the stile and turn right on the old packhorse way.

(3) Where the path forks, go right for 150yd to visit Lud's church; then return to the fork and continue descending right; eventually you cross a brook by a footbridge. Go over the adjacent wall stile and along the path to the left, to a former mill building. Go to the right of the building and up the drive. Cross the road junction and go along the farm drive. Pass round the right-hand side of the house and go through a gate: then follow the left-hand wall to a corner stile. Go over and follow a wall. At its end, swing right down the field to cross a stile/footbridge in the field corner. Cross the field and a wall stile just right of the house to reach a road.

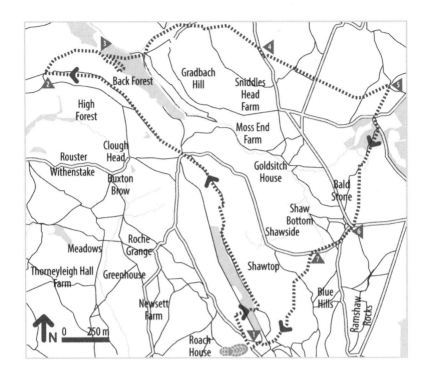

[4] Turn right, and after 80yd turn left over a stile, and over another in the wall ahead, then cross the field beyond. You will come to a walled track: follow this past a barn, and go along a rough path to a minor road. Go straight across, pass the house, go through a gate, and follow the path along the fence to a wooden fence stile. Cross this and keep straight ahead along the wall to a gate; beyond this the path line is straight ahead to reach a farm road.

[5] Turn right, and continue to a road junction. Go down the road opposite for 100yd, then turn right on a wide path through trees; continue on a clear path across moorland to a wall gap adjacent to a large rocky outcrop. Go through the gap and turn left along the wall to the corner, before crossing the other side to find a clear path that ends at a road junction.

6 Take the road opposite, and at a fork go right to reach a stile/ gateway on the left.

7 Go over this and along a farm road to pass through a second stile/gate. In a short distance further on, go right over a stile on to a clear moorland path leading back to the start point.

Points of interest

The Roaches is a gritstone rock face much used by climbers. Lud's church is a rocky church that was used for secret worship by followers of the religious reformer John Wyclif, persecuted during the reign of Richard II.

Ilam and Grindon

START On the roadside in the village, or in the car park at Ilam Hall, DE6 2AZ, GR 134508

DISTANCE 10 miles (16km)

SUMMARY A fairly strenuous walk, but with an easy finish

MAPS OS Landranger 119

WHERE TO EAT AND DRINK The Tea Rooms at National Trust Ilam Park at the back of the Hall, T01335 350503, 11:00–16:00 but check seasonal opening

An energetic walk with steep gradients through attractive countryside.

1 From the drive entrance to Ilam Hall take the road uphill, opposite the school, and go over a stile on the left into the park. Follow the clear track to where it turns left; here veer right to join another track descending to a footbridge. Cross the bridge and head slightly right over the field through a stile in the wall. The route goes right over more stiles to a road near Rushley Farm. Turn left, follow the road around right to a house drive, and cross the adjacent stile. Climb the hillside, cross two stiles, and follow the right boundary wall across two fields; then go diagonally left to a corner stile in the next field. Cross this, and follow the left boundary to Slade House. Go to the right of the house and away along the drive to two small pools by a stile/gate. Cross this, and go diagonally left across the field to the corner stile and road. Go over the stile opposite and along the boundary wall, then over another stile and follow a steep descending path to the valley bottom. Cross the footbridge over the River Hamps on to the Manifold Trail.

2 Go through the kissing gate opposite, and take the track off right and through the gate. Go left where the track ends, along the field boundary and through a small gate in the corner. Turn right, and follow a path over several stiled/gated fields to reach a narrow road. Go right, and just before a farm take a footpath on the right: this is a diversion around the farm and joins the track again. Then go down through a gate at the bottom of the hill. Ascend to a stile in

the top corner, go through this and along field edges first, then to the right of a farm track to Grindon.

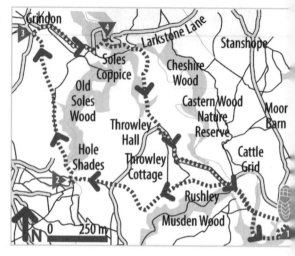

3 Follow the road right, downhill round a sharp left hairpin bend, and cross the stile on the right. Descend parallel to the right edge, and through the hedge at the bottom over a stile to the Manifold Trail at Weag's Bridge.

4 Turn right along the trail, and where it turns right, take the signed footpath on the left to go through a gate, across a field and over a bridge towards a farm. On approaching the farm, fork right up a steep gradient and follow the farm track through gates/stiles to the third field. Here, climb up left away from the track to a wall stile just to the left of a copse. Descend the field beyond towards Throwley Hall Farm, and through a stile into a small spinney adjacent to the farm. Go through this on to the road, and swinging left past the old hall ruins, steadily descend to Rushley Farm. From this point reverse the outward journey as far as the footbridge. Go over and right along Paradise Walk, which follows the river back to the village.

Points of interest

 The village church in Grindon is known as the 'Cathedral of the Moors'; inside there are two Saxon stone coffins.

Trysull and Claverley

START Near the school on Hunter's Green in Trysull, WV5 7HP, GR 851938

DISTANCE 11¼ miles (18km)

SUMMARY Easy

MAPS OS Landranger 138 and 139

WHERE TO EAT AND DRINK The Bell Inn in Trysull, www. holdensbellinntrysull.co.uk T01902 892871, 11:30am–3pm, 5am–11pm

A good walk with panoramic views.

1 Go left along the road to Crockington Lane. Turn right for about 350yd, to a footpath sign on the left. Go over the fence in the hedge gap, and cross the field on a bearing of 220 degrees to the remains of a hedge, and go across to the next hedge. In the next field walk towards a solitary tree (bearing 240 degrees), and head to the protruding corner of a hedge with a gap. Go through and along the left hedge to a broad green lane. Opposite, and slightly left, is a gap in the hedge. Go through and straight ahead to a pole, and keep on the same line to reach the B4176. Turn right and then left on a track waymarked as the Staffordshire Way, and keep going until you get to a T-Junction of tracks.

2 Turn right and follow the track to a road.

3 Go left, and in a short distance take a footpath on the right. Follow this path straight across Whittimere Farm to a stile, and head in a similar line across two fields to a stile near Admoor Cottage. Turn right to go around the cottage, and left along the road to a T-junction. Go left through Draycott and turn right by a half-timbered building along a minor lane. Follow this around a couple of sharp bends.

4 Turn left along another lane to Claverley.

5 Take the opportunity to explore the centre of the village, and then re-trace your steps back as far as a letterbox: go left through

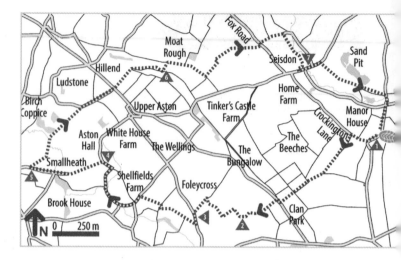

a small housing estate, until the road narrows to a track. Take the path crossing to Danford, a hedged path that widens and joins the elbow of a lane. Continue to the B4176, and by the Inn cross the road. Follow the path ahead, with the hedge on your right, to a stile. Go over and half right towards a pole half way up, and continue on the same line to reach a hunter's gate on the ridge top.

⑥ Go through and to the corner of the barn, then left to a gate on the farm drive. Turn right to reach a hunter's gate and a Staffs Way sign on the left. Follow this well signed path as far as the road near Woodcote. Turn left for a few yards, and then right along Post Office Road until you reach a stile on the right, opposite house No. 148. Go over the stile, and over two more, and follow the distinct path along the bottom of gardens on the edge of Seisdon. The path continues to the last house on a bend, where a stile on the left reaches a minor estate road.

⑦ The path goes through a garden to the road near Smestow Brook bridge (or keep on the road, then left and left again to the bridge). After the bridge you reach a green lane on the right. The lane will bring you to The Mill, The Bakehouse, and a road in Trysull. Go right and cross the road by the church back to the school.

Bramshall and Loxley Hall Parkland

START The village hall at the end of Church Croft; there is car parking available around the church area, ST14 5BG, GR 061332

DISTANCE 8 miles (11.8km)

SUMMARY Easy

MAPS OS Landranger 128

WHERE TO EAT AND DRINK The Olde Bramshall Inn, www.bramshallinn.co.uk, T01889 563634. Also The Robin Hood, www.robinhoodbramshall.com, T01889 566032, Mon–Thur 12–3pm and 5–11pm, Fri–Sun 12–10pm; and Strawberry Farm Garden Centre Coffee Shop & Dining Table, www.strawberrygardencentre.com, T01889 562292, Mon–Sat 9–5pm, Sun 10.30–4.30pm

A circular walk through rural landscapes and parkland.

1 From the village hall take the path into the churchyard, and go left down a path to cross the B5027 into Bennett's Lane. At the level crossing take the footpath right, alongside the railway, and go into a field, shortly bearing left to a footbridge. Continue through woodland to a stile. Walk up the next field, veering left to a gate and on to the A518. Turn right. On the bend take a footpath on the left up an entrance to a field. Follow the track through a gate, and then follow the edge of the woodlands to a wooden stile. Cross into the woodland and go right to reach a gate at a house. Go through and turn left down the drive on to a lane, where you turn right.

2 In a short distance take a footpath on the right through a gate, and another gate on the left. Follow the right boundary around the corner of the field to find a wooden stile near a belt of trees. Cross this and follow the belt of trees on your right to cross fields and more stiles to the end of the trees. Continue in a similar direction to reach a lane at a sharp corner, and go off right along this to reach the A518. Cross this on to a wide track. Follow the track and continue straight on through woodland. Beyond a house keep to the hedge on your left, and after about ¼ mile you will reach a metal gate in the right corner of the wood. Go through and follow

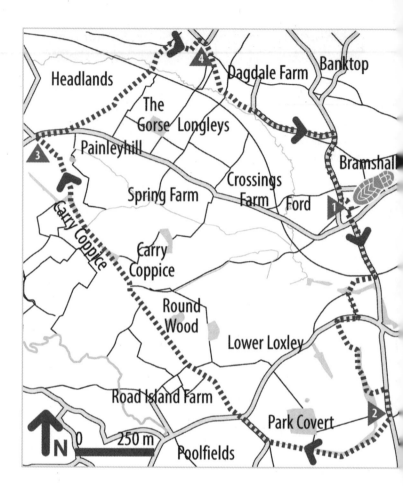

the left hedge and a track straight across a field to reach the B5027 road.

③ Turn right. Shortly take a signed footpath on the left, opposite a farm. Bear right through the field, and then follow the left hedge to a wooden stile. Cross this, and another one, and follow the left hedge to where it turns left. Cross the field straight ahead to a gate. Go through. The route follows a similar direction across the farm track, the next field, more stiles, over the railway and a footbridge beyond. It then follows the right-hand boundary and through a gateway. Bear right to a stile near the hedge corner. Cross this, and the next field to cross a stile. Turn left, and leave the field on to a lane.

④ Turn right, and right again on to a track towards a house. Take the path through the double gates on the right and cross the field to the diagonally opposite corner. Here, cross the stiles and footbridge, and follow a hedge on the right to another stile. Cross this, and go left to pass through a small complex of buildings; at the end of these continue along the drive to meet a lane. Turn right to a T-junction, and turn right again, back into the village and to your starting point.

Points of interest

Bramshall is a pleasant rural village consisting of farms, old buildings, a church, modern housing and a good range of facilities.

Loxley Hall is now a special school owned by the county council. It is an early nineteenth-century house and listed building.

Longnor, Hollinsclough and Pilsbury

START The market square/car park, Longnor, SK17 0NT, GR 088649

DISTANCE 10 miles (16km)

SUMMARY Moderate

MAPS OS Landranger 119, Explorer OL24

WHERE TO EAT AND DRINK Ye Old Cheshire Cheese in Longnor, http://theoldecheshirecheese.co.uk, To1298 83218. The Pack Horse Inn in Crowdecote, www.thepack-horseinn.co.uk, To1298 83618, Wed–Sun food served 12–2.30pm, and until 9pm in the evening. Also in Longnor, Cobbles Café, www.cobblescafe.co.uk, To1298 83166, Thurs–Sun 8.30am–4pm (-ish)

An invigorating walk through diverse scenery with many historical associations.

① With the market square on your right, set off over the crossroads. Shortly bear right along a minor road (not down the hill), and follow the footpath to Fawside. Go down, across the River Manifold, and up to meet a road. Turn right for ¼ mile, and go right at the junction. Follow a lane up, and shortly after a small S-bend, cross the stile on the right. Cross fields up to a stile in the top wall on to Fawside Edge Farm drive and the road. Go over the stile opposite. Follow the boundary wall over three more stiles to reach a narrow lane. Turn left, then right at the junction, and descend along a stony-walled track to Hollinsclough.

② On reaching the road in Hollinsclough go straight over, and after ¼ mile, take the track to the left just before a right-hand bend. Cross over the cattlegrid, and follow the track. After ¼ mile take the right fork. Cross the footbridge over the River Dove.

③ On reaching the road, turn right to Glutton Bridge. Here turn left, and almost immediately right, and follow the lane to meet the green lane beyond Underhill. Cross the green lane and go over stiles to Crowdecote. Pass the Packhorse Inn and turn left down a lane. Follow the lane and path across fields to the remains of Pilsbury Castle.

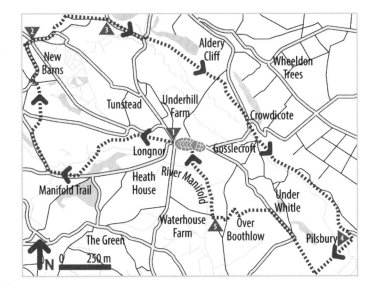

(4) Take the lane down right to Pilsbury, and cross the River Dove; then head up the bank to the road. Turn right for ¾ mile to a left turn; go down this lane for about 200yd, and through a gate on the right to head down the field along a track as it 'S-bends' down to a farm. Follow the arrows straight through the farmyard, and leave it by a made-up track. In about 100yd you come to a stile set in the middle of nowhere.

(5) Cross this, heading right, and follow the squeezers along the banks of the River Manifold towards Longnor. Finally head up the slope towards a farm and the village. At the road turn left to regain the market place.

Points of interest

Pilsbury Castle consists of the motte and bailey remains of a Norman castle.

Hollinsclough: the packhorse train and bridge close to the village are an old silk route from Liverpool. Silk buttons were made in the area.

Ilam and Alstonefield

START The roadside in Ilam, DE6 2AZ, GR 135508

DISTANCE 9 miles (14.5km)

SUMMARY Moderate

MAPS OS Landranger 119

WHERE TO EAT AND DRINK National Trust tea rooms, Ilam Hall, 10.30am–5.00pm; The George in Alstonefield, www.thegeorgeatalstonefield.com, T01335 310205

A grand tour of the area.

1️⃣ Take the road towards Dove Dale from the memorial, and find a footpath sign on the left and a gate. Go through. Ignore the path to Dove Dale going right, and take the track going left of the hill. This becomes a clear path along the boundary wall, and climbs steeply to a corner stile on the left, partly hidden from view by a tree. Go over and take a diagonal line across the field. Go through the second gate on the left to a wall stile just left of a barn. Go over and turn left, then turn right on a track which passes through Air Cottage grounds; reach a ladder stile by a wood. Follow the clear but narrow path through the wood as it wends its way down to the river in Dove Dale.

2️⃣ Cross the river and turn left for a delightful walk on an easy path which follows the river to the hamlet of Milldale. Take the lane between cottages; it climbs steadily to Alstonefield.

3️⃣ Turn left at the green in front of the pub, then keep left where the next road merges from the right. It is shortly followed by another junction, beyond which turn immediately left again on to a track by a house. Go over a stile. Follow the boundary wall and the well defined path that descends steeply to a road. Go right for about 300yd, and left over a stile. Follow the path, which turns sharply right up the slope to a stile. Cross this, and the one over the road, and follow the wall up the field. Go over two stiles before angling slightly left to pick up a clear path ascending the field along a wall to arrive at a narrow track. Cross straight over on a clear path to a wall stile.

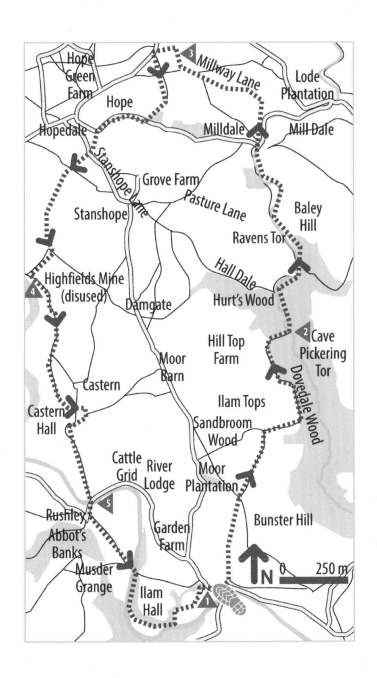

Hope Green Farm

Hope

Hopedale

Hope

Stanshope Lane

Grove Farm

Pasture Lane

Milldale

Mill Dale

Lode Plantation

Stanshope

Baley Hill

Ravens Tor

Hall Dale

Highfields Mine (disused)

Damgate

Hurt's Wood

2 Cave Pickering Tor

Moor Barn

Hill Top Farm

Castern

Castern Hall

Ilam Tops

Sandbroom Wood

Dovedale Wood

Cattle Grid

River Lodge

Moor Plantation

Rushley

Abbot's Banks

Musder Grange

Garden Farm

Ilam Hall

Bunster Hill

N   0   250 m

1

3 Millway Lane

4

5

④ Go through and left to follow the hillside path, passing the remains of lead mines, to where it ends at a wall corner. Cross the stile and turn left, then curve right to descend to a gate/stile in the far right corner. Follow the path along the edge of the next field, and through to the access road round Castern Hall. Go along the road past the hall; you can leave it and take a shortcut over a stile and round the slope, where you rejoin it.

⑤ A few yards further on leave the road on a path angling down the field in a direct line for Rushley Bridge, seen ahead. Find an obscured stile, and go through and cross the bridge. In 50yd turn left over a stile, to reach a wall stile. Go over and up the small slope. Go through the gate ahead, from where the way ahead is easily seen crossing the river by a footbridge. Turn right on to Paradise Walk, a delightful scenic path to Ilam Hall from where you take a path past the church back to the village.

Kidsgrove Circular

Start The car park in Meadows Road, Kidsgrove, ST7 1BU, GR 839544

Distance 8 miles (13km)

Summary Easy

Maps OS Landranger 118

Where to eat and drink There are various pubs and establishments in the area

An easy walk with interesting, mainly urban scenery.

1 From the car park, turn right into Station Road and cross the A50 on to some spare ground to reach the track of the former Potteries loop line. Turn left on to this disused railway, and follow it through the remnants of a colliery, gently arcing to the right, and passing under a lane; continue along the track, which becomes the landscaped Tunstall Greenway. Cross a road and go through a cutting, and keep going behind terraced housing until you reach Scotia Road. Turn left, and take the second road on the right.

2 In a short distance take a pedestrian greenway on the left. Take the first fork right, and follow this greenway to cross Westport Road and the A5271; eventually you will reach Westport Lake Road, which shortly crosses a canal.

3 Here go down to the right, and follow the towpath for approximately 3½ miles, until you reach Harecastle tunnels. Go up the steps between the two tunnels and on to Chatterley Road. Turn left along the road; soon you will reach the junction with Hollywall Lane.

4 Here bear right, then immediately left on to Boathorse Road; this becomes a track. At the junction at the top of the incline turn right, and continue straight ahead down Nelson Bank and along Boathorse Road. At the junction with The Avenue turn right, then take the second left to Meadows Road and the car park.

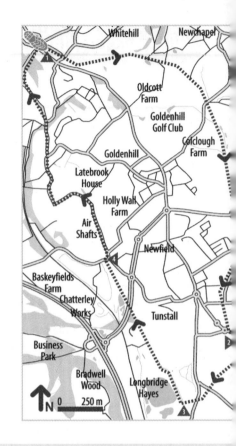

Points of interest

 Greenway is a dismantled loop line which has been converted into this pleasant walkway.

The Trent and Mersey Canal was constructed by James Brindley and opened in 1777.

The Harecastle tunnels: the original tunnel is on the left and was also constructed by Brindley. The disused canal now passes through the Thomas Telford tunnel.

OTHER WALKING GUIDES FROM CROWOOD

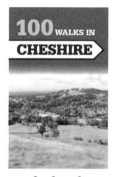

978 1 78500 181 9

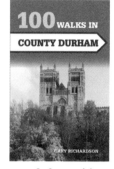

978 78500 306 6

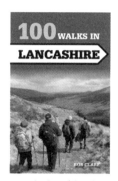

978 1 84797 899 8

978 1 78500 183 3

978 1 78500 302 8

978 1 78500 043 0

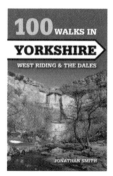

978 1 84797 909 4